Afriats

◆

Understanding Forced Interpersonal Interactions

Richard Bird Baker

iUniverse, Inc.
New York   Bloomington

Afriats
Understanding Forced Interpersonal Interactions

iUniverse books may be ordered through booksellers or by contacting:

iUniverse
1663 Liberty Drive
Bloomington, IN 47403
www.iuniverse.com
1-800-Authors (1-800-288-4677)

ISBN: 978-1-4502-6331-3 (sc)
ISBN: 978-1-4502-6332-0 (ebk)

Printed in the United States of America

iUniverse rev. date: 11/15/2010

This book is dedicated to the memory of James Howard Baker, who always stood on his own feet, always giving and never asking a thing from others, and to the memory of Evelyn Bird Baker, who always stood beside him through the hard times and the glad times, accepting a life of hard work and sacrifice for her children.

I would like to thank the people who helped me with the computer technology involved in writing and submitting this book: Diane Stinger, Lonnie Baker, Aaron Feild, Don and Diana Hartman, Matt Dela Mura, and Jacque Evanson.

Other books available by Richard Bird Baker through iUniverse are:
Affriation Phobia
Letters from Across the Big Divide
Corral Dust from Across the Big Divide

Contents

INTRODUCTION

This may be one of the most important books you will ever read. It identifies, defines, describes, analyzes, and suggests actions to take toward an extremely widespread social phenomenon, one that professional social scientists should have identified at least a century ago. Somehow the social scientific community has overlooked this phenomenon, which I find surprising, because it is one that affects, if not envelopes, the vast majority of people in modern society. This social phenomenon is likely one of the leading causes of stress, fatigue, frustration, disappointment, disillusionment, depression, unhappiness, anger, quarrels, road rage, violence, substance abuse, domestic abuse, neurosis, and perhaps even suicides in modern civilization. I am referring to the phenomenon of *afriations*.

Don't bother to look that term up. Hopefully it will someday be defined in our dictionaries, but at the time of this writing, it must simply be described as a term I have coined. I am presenting, please remember, a concept that is yet to be identified academically, so of course it has not been assigned a name. This coined word and a few other related terms I needed to coin will promptly be defined and explained in this book's first chapter.

I am not a professional social scientist. Nor am I a behavioral psychologist, M.D., Ph.D., D.D.S., or any other kind of institutional-academy achiever who has earned the right to be referred to as "Doctor." I realize that in the minds of many people, this is probably detrimental to my credibility. I truly have a great deal of respect for people whose studies and contributions to knowledge have earned them a doctorate. However, let's realize that a very intelligent and motivated high school graduate can normally earn the title "Doctor" in eight years. I have studied and closely observed society's afriations for over three decades and I'd humbly suggest I am likely the world's foremost, if not the world's only, authority on the phenomenon of afriations.

To be fair, I should mention that most of the principles and beliefs expressed in this book result from personal observation, analysis, and interpretation, and not from any form of systematized scientific research. I am no longer young, and my remaining lifetime may be too brief for extensive research. Anyone who is interested enough to conduct a controlled research project to verify or discredit any of my points is certainly welcome to do so.

In the mid-nineteen eighties, I worked from fifteen to twenty hours a week for almost three years on a book that presented all the concepts described in this book. I wrote the book as a psychological novel, believing this literary genre would be the best vehicle to communicate my social philosophy. I sent copies of the manuscript to numerous publishing companies, large and small. I actually received considerable earnest praise from a number of associate editors and marketing agents for the book's literary and social merit.

However, they all told me that neither literary merit nor social merit was selling books at the time, and that my book most likely wouldn't sell for them either. I was continually told my novel was too "experimental," that there was no substantial market for "experimental fiction," and that I should "stick to genre fiction where the market for book sales is stronger." Twenty-one years later, I decided that I should have written these concepts in a nonfiction format, one that readers might refer to as something like a "pop psychology," "pop sociology," or "pop self-help book." I don't know how to classify this book. I'd hate to be a librarian wondering where to shelve it. I'll just say it is the result of converting my original novel to a nonfiction format, with the benefit of an additional twenty-one years of observation and deliberation on the subject. If this book helps any readers to recognize, cope with, or avoid the kind of afriations that cause many people grief, it will have served its intention.

1

THE SEVEN INTERACTIONAL CATEGORIES

Historically, people have been classified in countless ways, all, of course, from the point of view of the classifier and for his or her specific purposes. People have been classified as males, females, Caucasians, Africans, Asians, Europeans, Democrats, Republicans, white collar workers, blue collar workers, vegetarians, meat eaters, hunters, gatherers, agrarians, nomads, right handers, left handers, right wingers, left wingers, Christians, Moslems, heathens, aristocrats, paupers, carpenters, writers, fishermen, servants, rulers, athletes, spectators, drivers, pedestrians, handicapped persons, bilinguals, philanthropists, thieves, homeless, foreigners, actors, engineers, law makers, law enforcers, youths, elders, students, educators, blonds, red heads, native Americans, white Anglo Saxon protestants, service workers, factory workers, herdsmen, cowboys, easterners, northerners, southerners, gays, straights, short people, tall people, fat or thin people, and by thousands of other labels which systematically categorize all of us by specific traits. Useful as these labels may be for their particular purposes, they are not adequate for or even relevant to our consideration of interpersonal interactions.

Within the context of interpersonal interactions, there are only seven categories of human beings that need concern us. Each of these seven classifications may contain people from any race, creed, nationality, or ethnicity, or any describable body type, occupation, or life style. As with any system of classification, these seven categories are all from the point of view of the classifier, whom I will simply refer to as "you" or "we' throughout this text. These seven categories are all based on people's social roles toward us, more specifically, the kind of interactions we either choose to have or are forced to have with them. I'll hereafter refer to these as the *seven interactional categories*.

Let's briefly list and define these seven categories. Each classification will be elaborated on in the following chapters. For now, this listing will merely serve to put all members of the human race in perspective.

The interactional category this book will largely focus on is called *afriats*, an acronym I created which stands for *acquaintance of forced regular interactions*. More specifically, an *afriat* is a person whose company we would not willfully choose, but with whom we are forced to interact regularly, frequently, or extensively by an organization, institution, or situation. It is pronounced af-free-ut, with a short "a" and a short "u" and with the accent on the first syllable. It is strictly a coincidence that this acronym's first two syllables are also the first two syllables of the word "Africa." The term has nothing to do with that continent, its inhabitants, or its descendants. An afriat may be a person of any race, creed, ethnicity, or geographical location.

Three related terms from the same root also need to be introduced and defined. An *afriation* is an organization, institution, setting, or situation that establishes or perpetuates frequent interactions between persons who would not voluntarily choose each other's company. In the pronunciation of this collective noun, the accent falls on the third syllable, which is pronounced with a long "a." The term may also be used to express the condition of being institutionally forced to interact with someone with whom one would not choose to associate, such as in the statement, "His afriation to Charles led to frequent friction."

The transitive verb *afriate* is pronounced almost the same as the noun afriat except of course for the long "a" in the third syllable. An example of its use would be in the sentence, "Henry's job afriates him to seven co-workers." Add a "d" to that verb and we form the adjective *afriated*. The accent again falls on the first syllable and the "a" of the third syllable is long. An example of how this adjective might be used is, "Henry is afriated to Fred through his job." The antonym for this adjective is the word *unafriated*, which describes a person who has no afriats.

The main focus of this text will be on the category afriats, but to put this category into perspective and to consider our alternatives to afriations, we must define and keep in mind the other six interactional categories. By far, our largest interactional category is that of our *irrelevants*. As the term suggests, irrelevants are people with whom we seldom if ever interact and whose actions don't noticeably affect our lives. Persons whom we never meet but whose actions significantly affect our lives for better or for worse comprise the third interactional category, our *effectuals*. Then there are people with whom we interact only once but whose encounter significantly changes the course of our lives. I refer to this fourth category as *single-contact influentials*.

Persons with whom we interact only occasionally, voluntarily or otherwise, comprise our fifth interactional category, that of *occasionals*. *Friends* comprise the sixth category, and can be defined as persons with whom we voluntarily associate to share mutual interests, activities, or affections. The seventh category I've simply labeled *enemies*, people who would knowingly and intentionally harm us or our loved ones, steal or vandalize our property, or thwart our intentions.

In addition to these seven interactional categories, there are *two auxiliary classifications* of people we must recognize. The first auxiliary classification is that of *pidocas*, an acronym I coined from the phrase *person in defiance of a categorical assignment*. All the vowels are short and the accent falls on the second syllable. These are persons we have mentally assigned to a specific category who endeavor to make themselves members of another category against our will, such as an afriat who endeavors to be a friend or an irrelevant who endeavors to be a single-contact influential. The second auxiliary classification of people is that of *aspirats*. The word is pronounced like the word "aspirin" except for the final "t." These are the specific individuals whom pidocas aspire to recatagorize. For an example, suppose Joe mentally classifies Ted as an afriat. If Ted insists on classifying Joe as a friend, Joe is Ted's aspirat and Ted is Joe's pidoca.

Pidocas and aspirats are all primarily members of one of the seven interactional categories and don't comprise an interactional category in themselves. As the term "auxiliary" implies, these two terms frequently prove very helpful when discussing the nature of afriations.

I find that these seven interactional categories are the only ones needed to discuss humanity in terms of social interactions. Although at first glance these classifications may seem like an over simplification, I cannot think of any individual who doesn't conveniently fit into one of these seven simple categories. If anyone can think of any exceptions after reading the ensuing chapters, please advise me of them.

When I'm explaining the principles of afriations, I find I need to constantly refer to the principles of the other six categories, sometimes quite in depth. So before we begin to discuss afriations at length, it's crucial that we examine the other six categories more thoroughly.

2

IRRELEVANTS

From the perspective of any given person, the vast majority of this planet's inhabitants are members of the human category *irrelevants*, people with whom we never interact and who have no apparent effect on our lives. This category includes billions of people we never see or meet. It includes people we see occasionally or even daily but with whom we never interact. For example, someone we see daily riding the same bus we take to work is an irrelevant if we never interact with her or him. This category includes people we once knew but with whom we have lost contact. It even includes former friends with whom we have had a falling out or in whom we have gradually lost interest, and with whom we no longer communicate.

Some people have raised objections to my idea of classifying most of the world's inhabitants as "irrelevant." They feel it conflicts with the accepted thesis that "no man is an island," and that "whatever fate befalls humanity befalls each of us." Of course, any fate that is substantial enough to affect humanity as a whole is certainly bound to affect each of us as individuals, but the converse is not true. No matter how concerned we are with humanity, no matter how much compassion we have for mankind, the actions and fate of most individuals on earth don't affect us any more than our actions or fortunes affect them.

In general, being a mutual irrelevant with someone is a convenient and favorable relationship. There is a certain comfort in knowing that our irrelevants don't require our interaction. Indeed, an irrelevant is someone we can normally ignore if we choose. Unlike an afriat with whom mutual interactions are institutionally required, we are normally free to walk away from any irrelevant who confronts us in person or to hang up on one who invades us by telephone. Irrelevants who attempt to place themselves in one of our other six interactional categories against our will place themselves in the auxiliary classification of *pidocas*, as we will discuss in more detail in Chapter Eight. Irrelevants who choose to become our pidocas can normally do so only if we allow it, except, of course, in extreme cases where legal authorities might have to be called on to restrain a relentless pidoca.

Normally, however, we have the comfort of knowing that irrelevants can be largely disregarded. If an irrelevant offends us on the street, for example, it's senseless to respond. Why waste time quarreling with someone we may never see again or with whom we are not required to interact? An old western adage advises, "Just because a jackass brays at you doesn't mean you have to bray back." Of course, if the irrelevant physically assaults us, he is no longer someone we can ignore. The assailant is now an *enemy*, not an irrelevant. We will discuss enemies in more detail in Chapter Five.

This is not to say that I am advocating we always behave coldly and indifferently toward all strangers. Strangers have helped me many times. Likewise, I normally stop for stranded motorists and frequently give rides to hitchhikers. I'm usually happy to give assistance or directions to strangers on the streets. But although I personally believe in being a good Samaritan, there is a comfort in knowing we have a choice between acknowledging or disregarding any of our irrelevants.

Most of us on occasion observe an irrelevant to whom we are attracted, and we aspire to categorically change the relationship from irrelevant to friend. If common interests, activities, or mental or physical attractions are substantial, of course, irrelevants often enter the category of friends quite naturally. If these mutual interests or attractions are not apparent, and if we don't have a mutual friend to introduce us to the irrelevant we wish to befriend, of course the change in categories is going to be more difficult to achieve. Unsolicited attempts at friendship, of course, may make us the irrelevant's pidoca instead of initiating a friendship, but I suppose it's a matter of nothing ventured, nothing gained. If we are outgoing enough to initiate a conversation with an irrelevant to see where it leads, we normally have nothing to lose and hopefully a friendship to gain.

I'm certainly not qualified to offer advice on how to befriend a reluctant irrelevant. There have been other books written on the subject, but that question is not really within the scope of a book intended to focus on afriats. For our purposes, there is nothing more that needs to be said here about the category of irrelevants. When we begin to discuss afriations in depth, it will be important to keep the principles of irrelevants in mind to better understand the nature of afriations and its alternatives. The two main characteristics of irrelevants, remember, are they are people with whom we never interact and whose actions don't noticeably affect our lives.

3

EFFECTUALS

I've known some very intelligent people who believe there is no such thing as luck. A person's fortune, they maintain, is brought on by his or her own choices, plans, and endeavors. Their beliefs could be summed up as, "Your life is what you make it."

I've known other people whose motto could be stated as, "Your life is what you make it—until somebody else messes it up for you." They maintain that in spite of all our plans and efforts, factors beyond our control and often beyond our awareness can dramatically affect our fate. These factors include major acts of nature, be they beneficial or disastrous. These factors also include people we never meet and with whom we never directly interact, but whose choices and actions produce either desirable or adverse effects on our lives. I've named this interactional category *effectuals*.

As with irrelevants, we never interact directly with effectuals. Most often we never see them, except perhaps via the media. Unlike irrelevants, whose actions don't affect us, effectuals often yield an enormous influence over our fate. This human category is relatively small in number, but with the possible exception of afriats, they cause most people more problems than any of the other six categories.

Effectuals have existed at least since ancient times. Imagine that we are ancient farmers or herdsmen in the Middle East and well accustomed to the rules, policies, and practices that our forefathers had been subjected to for generations, those established by effectuals called "kings." One day an army from a distant city named Rome arrives to announce that an emperor has decided that all the inhabitants of this land should be his subjects, live by his rules, and pay him heavy taxes. The Roman Emperor would now be our primary effectual.

The United States of America became an independent nation when some colonial leaders decided not to abide by the policies and taxes imposed on them by their effectuals in England. Of course, there were colonialists who were adverse to the idea of independence, the "Tories." From their perspective, the promoters of the American Revolution, men like Thomas Jefferson, were adverse effectuals. In less than three decades, sign language interpreters for Meriwether Lewis were attempting to explain to the Northern Plains Native Americans that an effectual across the big pond named Napoleon had chosen to conduct large-scale warfare in Europe. Needing more money, Napoleon had decided to sell this land that French effectuals claimed they owned to Thomas Jefferson, their new primary effectual, who resides far beyond the rising sun. This means, the natives were told, that all the "Indians" in what was then called "Upper Louisiana" were to be under the dominion of the great white father in Washington. A number of decisions made by the effectuals who followed Mr. Jefferson quickly led to the near extinction of the crucial plains buffalo, to the dividing of the west into farms, ranches, and towns, to the near extinction of the aboriginal residents, and to transplanting the surviving native people to mandatory reservations.

This is only one of the thousands of historical examples of the power of effectuals to totally alter a population's life style or to even threaten its very existence. In fact, it could be said that the recorded history of mankind is largely a series of accounts of the enormous impact that effectuals have imposed on the general population.

Although effectuals have been critically tampering with their subjects since the earliest days of recorded history, their numbers and their potential has never been as great as it is in today's modern, technological society often referred to as the "global economy." Historically, the most common role of an effectual was to send his armies to conquer and claim a region. At the time of this writing, 2007 A. D., this still occurs occasionally. Fortunately for me, my friends, my occasionals, my afriats, and my local irrelevants, no military conquest of a population has occurred in the region where I live for almost one hundred and thirty years, not since people like the Sioux, the Blackfeet, and the Cheyenne were defeated and reservationalized. Most of today's effectuals carry out their widespread influences with nonmilitary tactics. Although their tactics are less violent than those of conquest-oriented rulers, their effects are at least as profound and widespread as ever.

Today's major effectuals are more numerous than ever, due to potentials developed by an expanded media, rapid electronic transactions, computerized business, unlimited manufacturing capabilities, and other modern elements of this shrinking world's global economy. Of course, today's effectuals still include the world's national rulers, elected or otherwise. But a host of other effectuals who were unheard of in earlier times now invade our lives daily: corporate leaders whose decisions affect the price and availability of everything; city, county, state, and national lawmakers whose new laws continually redefine our legal limits; advisers and lobbyists who influence our lawmakers' decisions; manufacturers whose production can influence the earth's ecology and even its weather; owners of commodities such as oil whose decisions affect the economy of every country in the world; and trend setters in technology whose rapid succession of inventions and planned obsolescence forces people to continuously buy "updated" equipment.

The scandal of planned obsolescence isn't new. Social economist and writer Vance Packard was warning Americans about this postwar phenomenon in the early nineteen sixties. The neurosis caused by over abundant and over accelerated change—the "every time I learn to dance they change the music" syndrome—was explained brilliantly by social psychologist and writer Alvin Toffler in the early nineteen seventies. I'm certainly not saying anything original about accelerated change or planned obsolescence. But the rate at which our effectuals are forcing technological and social change has gone far beyond what Packard and Toffler predicted. One of the most obvious areas of this perpetual obsolescence is in the field of household computers. Personally, I've never been very knowledgeable about computer technology. I'm finding it enough of a challenge to word-process this manuscript. But people who attempt to keep up with the latest developments in computer innovations tell me they must purchase new components at least annually.

People often ask me, "What's the harm in a little social and technological change? Isn't change natural?"

Certainly change is natural and often healthy when it occurs gradually enough for people to adjust. But our effectuals have long gone beyond that pace. Humans are social animals and we all need to feel securely and appropriately situated in our culture. When our culture changes so frequently and so rapidly that many people are confused as to how they fit into it, personal and social disorder results. It's long been known that more than a small amount of neurosis and crime result from continually forced, rapid change. Far too much of this forced change has been executed for the profits of the effectuals producing the changes and not for the benefit of the people most affected by them.

It's hard to tell a person "your life is what you make it" when the whim of one or more effectuals can swiftly render her or his line of work obsolete. For an example, I have several old friends who are former professional musicians, most of them long ago having gained college degrees in music. They frequently remind me that a few decades ago, there was live music everywhere. Almost every supper club, dance club, night club, honky tonk, motel lounge, airport, truck stop, roadhouse and dive had live music playing on a band stand, often seven nights a week. The musicians frequently grumbled about having to play more commercial music than they preferred. Most of them wished they could be playing something like jazz, blues, bluegrass, folk, classical, or original music for a living instead of those redundant top forty hits, but at least they were using their trained skills to earn their living. In those days, the music business was strictly unionized. Work was plentiful and a full-time union musician earned about as much pay as a full-time union plumber or carpenter. Then the effectuals in our state legislature legalized machine gambling in places that had formerly hired live music. Other effectuals soon developed a spectacle called "karaoke" that is frequently conducted in places that formerly hired live music. Other effectuals came up with the idea of "sports bars" where spectators watch events on big screen television in establishments that formerly hired live music. Other effectuals developed and promoted more efficient sound equipment for disc jockeys. Within a decade, all my trained musician friends were delivering pizzas.

Of course, professional musicians aren't the only people who've been misplaced by the actions of effectuals. People who specialized in building or repairing carburetors recently became the victims of their effectuals who developed and promoted fuel injection. The effectuals who originally developed and distributed automobiles were probably not appreciated by wagon and buggy manufactures. Prevalence of the automobile resulted in more physical and social change than any early-twentieth-century inhabitant could have imagined.

In the early nineteen sixties, my father was considered the best television repairman in our town of sixty thousand residents. By the late sixties, his effectuals had created a demand for colored television, a phenomenon that confused and frustrated this man who'd become an expert at repairing black and white television sets. He decided to begin a new career in furniture upholstery at the age of sixty-four. Similarly, I've known self-employed auto mechanics whose careers were thwarted by their effectuals who developed the use of electronic computerization in automobile engines, changes that required the use of expensive computerized technology for diagnosis and repair, changes that required the work to be done in the shops of automobile distributors.

These are just a few examples of the countless incidents in which our effectuals' decisions have displaced skilled tradesmen nearly to the extent that the fencing of the western plains and the massacre of the buffalo displaced my region's original inhabitants. Right now I can hear some readers saying what people often say to me during discussions of this topic: "We have to keep up with the times, don't we? The times are changing, you know."

Let's get one thing straight: the times are *not* changing. The sun still rises and sets at the same time it did when the Romans conquered the Middle East. The earth still takes about three hundred sixty-five and one-quarter days to revolve around the sun. The moon still revolves around the earth in slightly less than thirty and one-half days. It still takes approximately twenty-four hours for the earth to make a complete rotation. Autumn still comes to my native region in Northern Montana in early September and winter still barges in on us in late October. Spring still comes to this cold land in late April and summer still drops by for a brief visit in late June and escapes in late August. Weather patterns on our planet are certainly changing due to our effectuals' inventions, but the times are not changing.

What do people mean when they declare, "The times are changing"? They actually mean *technology* is changing, and it's changing so unreasonably fast many of us can't keep afoot. A huge percentage of the new jobs on the market are created by new developments in technology. How can we expect a person to invest years in training, to say nothing of the financial investment, knowing that at any time this new technology can be rendered obsolete at the whim of some effectual?

In all fairness to effectuals, I'll be the first to admit that not all of their results have been adverse. Indeed, many of the finer things in life we benefit from and even take for granted have been endowed upon us by effectuals. They have created great music, art, and literature. They have abolished slavery and child labor. They have outlawed debtors' prisons and torture. They have brought us the comforts of plumbing, electric lights, and gas furnaces, to mention just a few things. I'd even go so far as to surmise that most of the effectuals whose actions have caused many people extreme inconvenience have acted out of good intentions. They simply gave more consideration to themselves and to the people they expected to benefit than to those they might displace.

When Henry Ford was creating assembly line manufacturing of the Model T, his intention was to free people from the efforts involved in keeping and utilizing horses. He did not foresee the congestion, pollution, and enormous physical and social changes that would result from widespread use of the horseless carriage. I'd surmise that most of our effectuals are decent people whose goals are to provide a good home and education for their children, financial security for their aging parents, and a few of life's luxuries for themselves. Many of them likely attend church and give to charities. It's not as if we were talking about a category of intentionally evil villains. But always recognize that one or more effectuals can unintentionally turn our lives upside down at any time.

The topic of effectuals entails one more aspect we need to consider. An effectual by definition, you will recall, is a person with whom we never interact but who affects our lives, for better or for worse, from a distance. A specific kind of effectual has emerged since the early twentieth century, and especially since the mid-twentieth century. The effectuals I am referring to have emerged with the development of the media, and I doubt if they could be anyone's effectuals without the media. For lack of a better term, I refer to them as *voluntarily-sought effectuals*.

How many teenagers in the mid-nineteen fifties adopted the rebel-without-a-cause, chip-on-the-shoulder attitude projected by James Dean on the silver screen? How many young boys imitated the military heroics of John Wayne in the movie "The Green Beret"? How many youths took on the image of oily hair with a huge wave in front, a ducktail in the back, and long side burns from Elvis like my friends, my afriats, and I did in junior high school? In the early sixties, the pop star image changed from greasy-haired rebels to all-American boys with crew cuts wearing penny loafers, white sox, and letterman sweaters, and in my high school yearbooks, we all looked like them. A few years later when The Beatles decided to grow shoulder length hair and dress as what the media had recently labeled "hippies," millions of us college-aged youths followed suit. Today, I'm at least thirty-five years out of touch with pop youth culture, but I'd suspect the fads of chains, spikes, flesh piercing, and green and orange dyed hair is done in imitation of voluntarily-sought effectuals.

Voluntarily-sought effectuals can influence more than faddish appearances. Drug oriented song lyrics of the late sixties influenced a lot of us to tolerate if not utilize recreational drugs. Lyrics of love and peace influenced the philosophies of millions of us during the late sixties and early seventies. One and a half decades later, the lyrics of satanic hatred and violence were suspected of influencing a number of youths found guilty of heinous crimes. I personally suspect that the angry, hateful, and violent cursing of gangster rappers I constantly overhear blaring from car windows in large cities reinforces if not causes urban gang and gun mentality.

But voluntarily-sought effectuals often contribute to society in a positive way. Michael Jordan's posters urging children to read more, posters of Michelle Kwan urging kids to practice better nutrition, Jerry Lewis raising funds for muscular dystrophy victims, James Brown calling on kids to stay in school, and Johnny Cash wearing black to protest what he considered an unjust war are a few examples. Media-oriented youths can be quite impressionable, and it seems that media managers as well as voluntarily-sought effectuals should never lose sight of their social responsibility.

For most people, voluntarily-sought effectuals pose no real problems. Unlike standard effectuals who can influence our lives against our will, voluntarily-sought effectuals can be ignored by simply ignoring the media that conveys them.

As I've previously mentioned, the main focus of this book will be on the interactional category of afriats. I have a good deal of advice I am anxious to share about coping with afriations. Unfortunately, I have been unable to acquire much self-defense against effectuals. I don't know if anyone has. I fall prey to them constantly in minor matters, and like many other people, I've had my life style, my work life, and my financial state seriously uprooted more than once by well-intended effectuals.

Of course, I try to do the obvious. I refuse to buy items that I suspect will soon be rendered obsolete. I try not to buy products from companies that I believe are negatively affecting my life, the lives of others, or the environment. I try to vote for the political candidates that I hope will have the least amount of negative effect on his or her constituents. But too often I find that I have voted for someone who ignores his or her constituents after being elected and serves only his or her self interests or the interests of financial supporters. Then I find myself working with groups that are trying to offset our effectuals' negative actions.

But all this helps very little. Even if all our elected officials were one hundred percent honest and competent, remember, the majority of our effectuals in today's global economy are not politicians. We experience a rather helpless feeling when the course of our lives is deflected by the actions of effectuals we can't identify, let alone control.

The study of effectuals should fill many volumes, for it should be an enormous social concern. But that is not within the scope of this book or my realm of expertise. For our immediate purposes, it is enough to remember that our effectuals are people with whom we never interact and probably never see, but who profoundly affect our lives for better or for worse.

4

SINGLE-CONTACT INFLUENTIALS

There are a few individuals whom we encounter only once, but who cause a drastic effect on our lives. I've named people of this interactional category *single-contact influentials*. Most of us encounter fewer than a dozen single-contact influentials in our lives. Indeed, I've met people, mostly small town or rural residents, who have never encountered one.

A personnel manager of a large business firm who hires us for a position and never sees us again is perhaps the most common example of a single-contact influential. A military recruiter who persuades a youth to join a branch of the armed services is the youth's single-contact influential. A businessman who persuades us to make a large purchase that requires years to pay for or the banker who approves of a large loan are single-contact influentials if we never see them again. A baseball talent scout who recruits a young prospect for professional minor league play is the youth's single-contact influential. A policeman who arrests us and a judge who sentences us also fit in this category.

Some people are affected very little by this category of people, and some are affected greatly. Unlike effectuals who can influence us enormously against our will, we can generally choose whether or not we wished to be affected by single-contact influentials. One exception to this would be someone who unintentionally causes us to be in a traffic accident or other mishap that has a long-term effect on our lives. Another exception, of course, is that we don't have any choice as to what an arresting policeman or a judge may decide about our fate once a crime is committed. Our only choice in this case is simply whether or not to commit the offense in the first place. But in most cases, an interaction with a single-contact influential is by choice, and so is our acceptance or rejection of what the individual offers us.

Very little needs to be said about this interactional category in a book that focuses on afriations. We simply need to recognize a single-contact influential when and if we encounter one and carefully evaluate the long-term consequences of his or her proposal. Is the offer something we really need? Will it prove to be to our benefit or will we later regret the long-term effects of the interaction? If we decide to forgo the interaction, the individual is not to be considered a single-contact influential; he or she remains an irrelevant.

5

ENEMIES

The fourth interactional category is that of *enemies*. Effectuals, you will recall, can often produce frequent adversities on our lives, but their effects are normally unintentional and sometimes unknown to them. Enemies, on the other hand, are individuals who would harm us knowingly and willingly. Their harm can take the form of physically injuring us or our loved ones, damaging or stealing our property, or intentionally thwarting our goals. Their motives may be sheer malice, revenge, or personal gain.

Probably the most crude, feared, and visible form of this category is our common street enemy. We live in a time when youth gang members are required to shoot an irrelevant from a moving car or beat an irrelevant on the street with a pipe to earn their feathers. Many people have long avoided walking through their neighborhoods after dark in fear of being robbed at gunpoint. A friend of mine living in a large western city was recently struck over the head while urinating in the restroom of a fast food restaurant and woke to find his wallet stolen. Such examples of enemy violence, of course, are commonplace. I've never been robbed at gunpoint, but several times I've been the victim of enemies who break into residences to steal valuables.

Of course, street thugs and robbers aren't our only enemies. I don't know whom I detest more, the thief who robs with a gun or the thief who robs with a pen, often under legal protection. Businessmen and professionals who devise "white collar" tactics to cheat their clients out of funds are no less despicable than thugs who would roll us in the streets.

People sometimes ask me, "What about liars? Are they enemies?"

I believe there are different levels of liars. I don't believe a person who lies to us to protect our feelings or the feelings of others is truly an enemy. Nor would I consider the person who lies about his accomplishments to make himself look more important a real enemy. But a liar who lies to deceive or cheat a person for personal gain is certainly an enemy, and they are probably more common than street thieves.

People who would intentionally thwart our intentions can be looked upon as enemies, even though their actions may be completely within the law. Enemies of this type often don't take their struggle with us personally. To them it's simply a case of two people having the same goal when there is room for only one person to achieve it. Business rivals, competing political candidates, or two persons rivaling over the same desired mate are among the most common examples of enemies endeavoring to thwart one another's intentions.

In the last few decades, we've seen more cases of enemy activity emerge in the world of competitive sports. I believe that sports in themselves are normally a healthy and productive pastime, but today our society takes them so seriously that enemy hostility often develops. Perhaps the most memorable example of this happened shortly before the 1994 Winter Olympics when Tanya Harding allegedly recruited a man to attempt to break the leg of her figure skating rival Nancy Kerrigan. At about the same time, a similar scandal occurred at the high school level when the mother of a teenaged girl trying out for cheerleading allegedly attempted to hire a man to kill the mother of a rival cheerleader, hoping the death of her parent would cause the rival to miss the cheerleading tryouts. I've observed numerous less severe incidents of former friends becoming enemies over a starting position on an athletic team. In short, enemies can emerge even in activities that were originally intended to be fun and in the interest of good sportsmanship.

Human beings have never been without enemies. Precivilized tribes often fought over hunting grounds or desirable campsites. Civilized history is marked with countless struggles over land and resources. Highwaymen have always robbed travelers and people have always rivaled over acquisitions. The question of what to do about enemies is at least as old as civilization itself. Many spiritual leaders, including Jesus Christ, have told us that the proper thing to do is to love them unconditionally. I have always considered myself a Christian, but I've never been quite the pacifist Jesus was. Loving my enemies won't stop them from hurting other victims. In regard to violent street enemies, many modern urban dwellers have resigned themselves to the practice of staying home behind locked doors. I personally believe that self-defense and retaliation, by individuals when possible or by society as a whole, is perhaps the only way to demonstrate that the actions of violent enemies are not to be tolerated.

Self-defense practices against white-collar business thieves and cheaters are harder to formulate. These enemies are often harder to identify and indeed often find legal protection for their offenses. My generation was taught to always read and understand the fine print before signing a binding contract, which is still good advice, but my generation's teachers didn't foresee the scams involving identification theft and computerized fraud that some of our enemies have cultivated today. I'm too out of touch with computerized financial practices to render any knowledgeable advice about these crimes.

As I've mentioned previously, the intent of this book is to examine afriations and to discuss ideas about coping with them, not to pretend I have any suggestions about how to ward off our enemies. But it was important to briefly discuss the category of enemies before entering our discussion of afriats, because unfortunately, many people tend to mistake afriats for enemies. That's a mistake that needs to be avoided but which is often hard to avoid without understanding the differences between the two categories.

6

FRIENDS

The fifth interactional category is most people's favorite, that of *friends*. These are the individuals with whom we voluntarily interact periodically if not frequently to share mutual interests, activities, or affections. This human category has *three subcategories*: *verified friends, unverified friends,* and *intimates.*

Verified friends are those whose relationship with us has survived an interpersonal crisis. The crisis may have been a highly heated dispute or just an accumulation of annoyances that make us wonder if the relationship is worth the trouble. If the friendship survives the crisis, normally it is because both parties have determined that the activities, interests, or affections involved outweigh the difficulties. Hence, a verified friendship is established. If the friendship does not survive the crisis, the two individuals involved become one another's irrelevants, occasionals, or in some cases, enemies.

Unverified friends are those with whom we've never faced a severe interpersonal crisis. Some friendships may never have to face one, and the relationship's interactions continue for years without major problems. For that reason, it's not valid to assume that verified friendships are necessarily more valuable than unverified friendships. If the relationship flows along smoothly for years without a crisis, perhaps it should be considered the most ideal kind of friendship. Just remember that it's not a crisis-tested, verified friendship yet, and that a crisis could produce unexpected results.

Intimates are friends with whom we can comfortably share many of our personal ideas and feelings. These are the people to whom we can tell our problems, hopes, fears, and certain secrets. Some people have no intimates; most of us have only a few. I don't know if it's possible to have more than a few at a time. Normally a person's intimates include only his or her spouse or "significant other," a few close relatives and/or a few close friends.

There have been many books written about how to gain and keep friends. That is certainly not the purpose of this book. But I'd like to suggest that I've never known a person of ample interests, activities, and human sentiment to be without friends. Most people I've met who have no friends have very few interests and activities in their lives and/or are just too cantankerous for most people's company. Those are problems that people can work on if they desire to gain friends. Of course, there are a relatively small number of people who feel they don't want or need friends.

Little more than this needs to be said about friends in a book that is concerned primarily with afriats. The principles outlined in this short chapter were necessary to mention, however, because many people tend to mistake afriats for friends, just as many people tend to mistake afriats for enemies. To do either can be a costly mistake, as we shall consider when we more thoroughly discuss afriations.

7

OCCASIONALS

The sixth interactional category is that of *occasionals*. As the name suggests, they are people with whom we interact occasionally and with whom we feel the interaction is not to excess. These interactions may be voluntary or they may be forced upon us by an organization, institution, or situation. In the case of a forced interaction, it is the *amount* of interaction required that distinguishes an occasional from an afriat. A person who comes to our place of work a few times a week to delivery a package and asks for a signature is clearly an occasional. The same person is clearly an afriat to someone else who sorts packages with him or her several hours a day. A landlord whom we see only when we pay rent or need repairs is our occasional. A landlord who lives on the premises and approaches us about domestic matters daily can be considered our afriat.

The difference between afriats and forced occasionals isn't always as clear-cut as in the two examples I just mentioned. For example, consider a delivery person with whom we are required to interact every workday. The interaction is certainly frequent. But if the daily interaction is limited to a short greeting, taking a package, and signing an invoice, I'd personally consider the delivery person an occasional. Someone else who, for whatever reason, may dread the delivery person's presence might prefer to think of him or her as an afriat. The same could be said about a bus driver who sells us a ticket daily or a waitperson who serves us several times a week. These people of frequent but very brief forced interactions can most easily be thought of as occasionals. Only in cases where we dread the interactions should they be thought of as afriats.

Most forced occasionals are easier to identify and categorize than the few gray-area examples I just mentioned. People we wait on or who wait on us once or twice a week are occasionals. Professional people we interact with on a regular but infrequent basis are occasionals: doctors, dentists, therapists, attorneys, councilors, clergymen, bankers, probation officers, financial advisers, insurance agents, and hair stylists are examples.

Besides having forced occasionals, we normally have occasionals with whom we interact voluntarily. They are normally people with whom we don't have enough in common to consider friends, but whom we don't ignore as we would our irrelevants. Neighbors we encounter briefly and exchange small talk with are occasionals, as are people we recognize in public places and casually chat with from time to time, whether or not we know their names.

When discussing occasionals, another gray area, one that is rather sensitive, needs to be considered. People often ask me, "What about old friends we rarely see any more? Are they still our friends, or are they now occasionals?"

When this occurs between two old friends, it is usually because the common interests and activities that originally bound them have waned, perhaps to the point where one or both parties no longer practice the activities. If the two parties no longer actively seek each other's company, I'd refer to them as occasionals, no matter how warm and reminiscent the interactions may be during their haphazard encounters. If they still get together on occasion to share lunch or a drink and conversation, I'd consider them old friends.

Remember, friends are people who voluntarily seek each other's company for reasons of mutual interests, activities, or affections. Sometimes two people who have no interests or activities in common become close friends simply because they like each other a lot. Old friends of this nature, especially if they have been or still are intimates, are more likely to plan a get-together periodically than old friends of waning interests. If extensive distance is the reason we rarely see an old friend, I still think of him or her as a friend no matter how infrequently we interact, especially in the case of verified friends.

When we begin to thoroughly discuss afriations, it'll be important to keep in mind the differences between afriats and forced occasionals. Remember, there are occasionals we interact with infrequently and those we interact with frequently but for very short periods of time. Even if the interactions are not pleasant, they are usually too limited to result in the kind of tension that frequently arises between afriats. Normally a smile and a little courtesy is enough to keep our interactions with occasionals pleasant.

8

PIDOCAS

The main focus of this book, of course, will be on the seventh and final interactional category, that of afriats. But before we are quite ready to consider afriats at length, let me remind you there are *two auxiliary classifications* of people in addition to the basic seven categories. Members of these two classifications are always primarily members of one of the seven basic interactional categories, which is the reason these two auxiliary classifications do not qualify as being interactional categories in themselves. The term "auxiliary classifications" is appropriate because it is often quite helpful to refer to these two classifications in a detailed discussion of the nature of afriations.

The first auxiliary classification of people is that of *pidocas*. As I mentioned in the first chapter, it is another word that needed to be coined. Like the term afriat, it is a convenient acronym. It is derived from the first letters of each word in the phrase *person in defiance of a categorical assignment*. Pronounce "pidoca" in three syllables with the accent on the second syllable "doc." All the vowels are intended to be short. Specifically, pronounce the vowel "I" as in the word "pin." Pronounce the vowel "O" as in the word "doctor," and pronounce the vowel "A" as in the word "tuna."

As we enter an interaction with an individual, we mentally assign that person to one of the seven interactional categories and we endeavor to interact from that perception. People who haven't yet read this book and thereby haven't begun to think of others as members of an interactional category still tend to assign other people to these categories subliminally. Most often these categorical assignments are mutual. The vast majority of our irrelevants think of us as irrelevants as well. The large majority of our friends think the same of us. Our occasionals normally perceive us as occasionals and our enemies usually feel the same bitter sentiments toward us as we hold for them. Even more afriats than not will think of us as afriats, at least subliminally if they are not familiar with the term.

Periodically, we all encounter individuals whose categorization of our mutual relationship differs from our own. A person who endeavors against our will to interact with us as if he or she were a member of a different interactional category is our pidoca. Let's briefly discuss a few of the most common examples of pidocas.

One of the most common types of pidocas are irrelevants who endeavor to become our friends or even our intimates against our will. People we encounter on the street who ask where we are going and try to accompany us against our will are pidocas. A man who continues to call a woman to ask for a date is her pidoca if she prefers that he remain an irrelevant. Likewise, former spouses or lovers with whom we now wish to be occasionals or irrelevants are our pidocas if they persist in trying to renew the relationship.

Persistent pidocas of this nature can be very pestering nuisances. They need to be told respectfully but firmly that we aren't interested in being more than occasionals, afriats, or irrelevants to them. That's usually all that's required, but in extreme cases, they can require a judge to issue a restraining order and even police officers to enforce it.

Irrelevants who endeavor to become our afriats are a little less common, but most of us encounter them occasionally. Uninvited missionaries who persist in coming to our doors to recruit us into religious organizations are examples of this type of pidocas. College fraternity or sorority members who continually visit student dormitories to recruit new members can be considered pidocas by students who have no interest in joining them. Irrelevants or occasionals who continually try to enlist us into any kind of organization or "work team" against our interests are pidocas.

Another commonly encountered type of pidoca is an irrelevant who endeavors to become a single-contact influential. Someone who attempts to persuade us to make a large investment against our interests is a pidoca. That includes salespersons selling costly items or investment advisors selling stocks or business shares. A person who attempts to recruit us into a branch of the military or into a civilian occupation against our wishes is our pidoca.

Pidocas sometimes exist even within the sub categories of the major seven interactional categories. Probably the most common example is the casual friend who endeavors to become an intimate against our will. This includes friends who insist on a sexual relationship with us when we prefer a platonic relationship. This also includes casual friends who want to know more about our intimate feelings and secrets than we are willing to share. If we want to preserve the friendship, pidocas of this nature need to be handled with more tact than our irrelevants or occasionals to whom we can ignore or simply tell to go away. But friends who become pidocas need to be made aware that such pursuits can and often do destroy a friendship and force former friends to think of them as occasionals or irrelevants.

People who are members of extensive afriations usually find that most of their pidocas are afriats. In a coming chapter, we will discuss this type of pidoca more in depth. For our purposes now, I'll just briefly mention that within afriations, we often find ourselves with afriats who endeavor to befriend us in spite of the fact that we share no common interests, activities, or affections. There are afriats who feel that everyone they are afriated to must be either "a friend or a foe," and that an afriat who doesn't readily accept their friendship is automatically an enemy. Afriats who endeavor to be our friends or enemies against our will are usually our most common pidocas.

Basically, there are two distinct types of pidocas we can expect to encounter. There are those who recognize, at least subliminally, their assigned interactional categories and respect their assigned categorical boundaries. Realizing that interactional categories are not static, such pidocas may make legitimate, tactful attempts to change their categorical assignment. Their approaches are usually pleasant and unthreatening. Sometimes their efforts are successful, as in cases where irrelevants, occasionals, or afriats become our friends. More often than not, their attempts aren't successful. Thoughtful pidocas can usually be told politely that we are not interested in their proposed categorical changes.

The second type of pidocas are those who simply don't recognize the boundaries of the category to which we mentally assign them. In their perception, we are mutually members of the category to which they have assigned us, a quite different category from the one we prefer. Annoyances often develop as they continually attempt to interact with us in ways we wouldn't expect from members of their assigned interactional categories. They are normally not as tactful as the first type of pidoca I mentioned. They tend to just barge into our categorization, invading all boundaries. Irrelevants, occasionals, and most commonly afriats who perceive us as friends or enemies are the most common examples of such pidocas. We will discuss afriated pidocas more thoroughly in a coming chapter.

Some pidocas can certainly be a major nuisance in our lives. Originally, I simply labeled this classification as "pests." This term, however, proved to be inadequate. Conversational use of the word "pest" is so widespread and generalized that we often apply it to persons who aren't attempting to change their assigned categories. For example, we might think of a valued, intimate friend as pestful at times when his activity is hindering our own. We might think of an occasional as pestful if he persists in holding longer conversations with us than we desire. We might think of an irrelevant as a pest if he panhandles us on the street. None of these pestful activities represents an attempt to change an interactional category. A new term was needed for a person in defiance of a categorical assignment; hence the acronym *pidoca* was created.

Remember, pidocas represent an auxiliary classification. All of our pidocas are primarily members of one of the seven main interactional categories, specifically, the category to which we intentionally assign them. Remember, the categorical assignments are our choice, not our pidocas'. And, of course, it is our choice if we eventually decide to change our minds. Interactional categorical assignments are often subject to change.

There have been numerous books written to teach assertiveness, a practice that is highly advisable for keeping pidocas within their assigned categories. Assertiveness training is certainly not within the scope of this book; nor am I highly proficient at it. However, it was necessary to define and examine the concept of pidocas before focusing on the nature of afriations.

9

ASPIRATS

In the last chapter, we defined *persons in defiance of a categorical assignment*, or *pidocas*. They are the people who attempt to ignore, challenge, or change the barriers of the interactional category we mentally assign them. The majority of these individuals will be cooperative when advised of our categorical intentions, but some can be unreasonably difficult.

Now let's look at pidocas from the opposite perspective, that is to say, from situations in which we ourselves are the pidocas. People's reaction to that suggestion is often, "Who, me? I'm not a pidoca! Who are you calling a pidoca?"

Let's face it, we are all pidocas on occasion, some of us infrequently, and some of us quite frequently. We all at times observe an irrelevant, an occasional, or an afriat whose talents, sentiments, appearance, or other attributes arouse a desire in us to categorize him or her as a friend. We are potentially a pidoca if he or she doesn't categorize us the same.

Actually, no matter how much we desire another person's friendship, we are not truly pidocas unless our aspirations are accompanied by genuine attempts to change the desired person's categorization. *Passive pidocas* is the term I give to all of us who yearn to befriend someone but make no effort toward that categorical change. We are *active pidocas*, the only true pidocas, only when we pursue or at least intend to pursue an interactional categorical change with the person who is the object of our aspirations. The person whom we aspire to affect is our *aspirat*.

The term *aspirat*, of course, is one I have derived from the verb "aspire." Don't confuse it with the existing noun "aspirant," which is a person who aspires to possess or achieve something. "Aspiration" is the noun we normally use in standard English for the object, person, or goal to which someone aspires. The term "aspiration" is too broadly used for our purposes because it refers to inanimate and intangible objects as well as people. *Aspirat* is the variation I've coined to label the person with whom a pidoca attempts to affect a categorical change. Except for the final "t," the noun is pronounced like the word "aspirin."

Aspirats comprise the second auxiliary classification of people. Like pidocas, all aspirats are primarily members of one of our seven main interactional categories. Most commonly, they are irrelevants, afriats, or occasionals.

I recently commented that I consider those of us who do nothing to affect the will of an aspirat to be passive pidocas, not true pidocas. A pidoca who attempts to influence the categorizing of an aspirat is an active pidoca, the only true pidoca because, by definition, a pidoca is someone who attempts to cross an aspirat's categorical barriers. A similar thing can be said about aspirats. Over the years, we may observe thousands of irrelevants, occasionals, and afriats that we imagine we would like to have a closer relationship with. Such aspirats might include *voluntarily-sought effectuals* we see only via the media. Unless we as pidocas are making an attempt to move in the aspirat's mind from a category such as irrelevant or afriat to one of friendship, the potential aspirat is merely what I refer to as a *passively-noted aspirat*. A true aspirat, one I refer to as an *actively-pursued aspirat*, is one whose pidoca is actively attempting to change the aspirat's categorical assignment.

Some people in our society do not find it difficult to approach an aspirat and express an interest in friendship. At times we notice them succeed. At other times they become annoying pidocas. Other people in our society, especially shy persons, perceive the intimidating categorical barriers to be impassible and never challenge them. Again, the best medicine I can think of for finding friends is cultivating ample interests and activities. Working on being more pleasant company is also a plus.

Many books have been written intended to teach a pidoca how to develop a close relationship with an aspirat. This is not the intention of this book and if it were, I'd be a poorly qualified pidoca to write it. But an understanding of afriations requires that we have a working knowledge of these two auxiliary classifications of individuals in addition to an understanding of the seven interactional categories. We have now concluded our required discussion of these categories, classifications, and related terms. We are ready to begin examining the history and nature of afriations.

10

AFRIATS

It may seem to some readers that most of this book's chapters thus far have ended in a cop-out. At the end of these chapters, I've continually found myself writing something to the effect of, "Many books have been written about how to interact with this particular interactional category. That is not within the scope of this book, nor am I qualified to offer much advice ...."

Our seventh and final interactional category allows me to write the opposite. To my knowledge, this is the first book written about afriats (except for my unpublished novel written in the mid-nineteen eighties). In fact, no word has previously been devised for the concept, at least not in the English-speaking world. I'd be very interested in knowing if any other language has a term for the concept. As to whether or not I'm qualified to expound on the subject of afriations, I'll let you readers decide.

I wish I could present a book full of research supporting my theories. All the principles presented in this volume are based upon my thirty years of observing, analyzing, and interpreting the nature, functions, and problems of afriations. If I were a few decades younger, I'd begin to conduct some lengthy surveys that would hopefully provide more credence to the views of society I am presenting. But although this is the first book written about afriations, I hope it will not be the last. Hopefully, publications of research on the topic will eventually follow.

As I mentioned briefly in Chapter One, the term *afriat* is one I needed to coin, for a collective term for the concept has always been absent in the English language. It is pronounced af-free-ut, with the spoken accent on the first syllable. The vowels "a" and "u" are short. It is an acronym for the phrase *acquaintance of forced regular interactions. Afriats* are people with whom we wouldn't normally choose to interact, but with whom we are required to interact extensively by an organization, institution, or situation. An *afriation* is an organization, institution, or situation that forces extensive interaction between people who otherwise wouldn't choose to interact. Recall also that the transitive verb *afriate*, pronounced almost the same but with a long "a" on the last syllable, means to cause extensive interaction between parties who would otherwise not choose to interact. Let's review also the adjectives *afriated*, meaning the condition of having afriats, and *unafriated*, the condition of having no afriats.

The most extreme example of an afriation I can think of is a prison. Let's imagine ourselves sentenced to spending twenty-four hours a day in a prison cell with about seven other afriats, never having a minute of privacy or solitude. Perhaps we eight afriats might be chained together daily, marched off to do forced labor while chained together, and marched back to our cells chained together every evening, never out of each other's presence. We'd know the feeling of being one hundred percent afriated.

Military basic training is another example of almost one hundred percent afriation. It's been over four decades since I personally experienced military training, and perhaps some things about it have changed since the early Vietnam Era. At that time, basic trainees spent nine weeks training together by day and sharing an open-bay barracks by night. The only brief moments of solitude I can recall were those of walking guard duty, a detail I frequently volunteered to do.

I recall that after basic training, life in the military allowed us more opportunities to briefly escape our afriats. Passes to town or access to recreational sites on post were very important to us, being our only legitimate chances to leave our extensive afriations for a short time. Threats of depriving us of those privileges were the most effective tools our officers and N.C.O.'s had in maintaining discipline.

In general, the more rank a serviceman accumulates, the more freedom he has to leave his afriation when he is off duty. At least that is true during peacetime. During periods of armed conflict, of course, he is subject to being sent to a battle unit at any time. Combat troops in an area of conflict again find themselves in a situation in which they are required to be in each other's presence one hundred percent of the time.

Prisons and military units are society's most extensive afriations, and interestingly enough, they were probably mankind's first afriations. We'll consider that concept more thoroughly in the next chapter, "The History of Afriations." For now, let's merely acknowledge that most modern afriations aren't quite as intensive as prisons or military units.

In modern society, by far our most common and widespread afriations are our institutions of employment. Larger companies with many employees are our best examples, of course, but small businesses with only a few employees can also be considered afriations if they continually force interaction between people who would normally not choose to share each other's company. Probably the second most widespread afriations are schools, public and private, including institutions of higher learning. Living situations often make afriats of people who might otherwise be irrelevants or occasionals. An institution such as a hospital, nursing home, or college dormitory might assign us roommates with whom we wouldn't voluntarily interact. We might answer an ad for housemates and move in with some residents whose company we otherwise wouldn't choose. We might live in an apartment building under circumstances that require us to interact frequently with residents whose company we otherwise wouldn't choose. These residents might be considered afriats if our interactions with them seem too frequent to consider them occasionals.

Remember, it's not only organizations and institutions, but also social situations that can afriate us. Afriats can simply be friends or relatives of friends. If we convene with someone frequently to share a common activity, that person is, by my definition, a friend. If said friend continually brings along a spouse, a "significant other," or another friend or relative who does not participate in the activity and perhaps has no particular interest in it, that person could be thought of as an afriat if the gatherings were frequent. Our spouse's relatives who come to stay with us too long or too often to be considered occasionals may be looked upon as afriats. If a high school boy goes to his girlfriend's house to visit her every time he hears her parents aren't home and always finds himself having to entertain her little brother, he might think of the little brother as an afriat.

The fact that no collective word has existed in English for an afriat until now illustrates two conditions: first, we are so conditioned to widespread afriation that we take the whole social phenomenon for granted; second, we don't recognize the social impact of this pervasive phenomenon. Of course, there have always been many terms used to refer to specific kinds of afriats: work colleagues, comrades, barracks mates, classmates, shipmates, platoon mates, team mates, school mates, cadre, cell mates, inmates, supervisors, servants, employees, squad members, and staff members are only a few examples. But until now, no collective term has ever been devised, at least in the English language, to refer to afriats in general or to the phenomenon of afriation. An examination of the history and the nature of afriations may help us understand why.

11

THE HISTORY OF AFRIATIONS

Comparatively speaking, our species is quite new. Geologists estimate our planet is approximately four and one half billon years old, and astronomers consider our Earth a comparatively young planet. We Homo sapiens have been evolving on our planet for only two million years, quite a short time compared to the history of many other species.

For most of those two million years, our evolving ancestors existed as small bands of nomadic hunters and gatherers whose constant migrations were dictated by the availability or lack of food and by the seasons. Until as recently as six thousand years ago, virtually all human beings were wandering tribesmen. As recently as one hundred and forty years ago, large and small tribes of hunters and gatherers still flourished on at least four continents. I've met some brilliant people who can make convincing arguments that our species was intended to exist as nomads and should have remained as such. Nevertheless, two social phenomena served to divert our existence from that nomadic lifestyle of not so long ago to the complex, mechanized social culture of today: civilization and the industrial revolution.

Of course, our prehistoric, wandering ancestors had no written language and recorded no accounts of their history. Our limited knowledge of them comes via artifacts and fossils. We know enough, however, to deduce that no afriations existed in prehistoric times unless we consider these prehistoric bands to be afriations in themselves. I don't know, nor am I aware if anyone knows, to what extent prehistoric people were free to leave a band or welcome to join another. It is known that many tribes throughout the world used banishment as punishment. This might indicate that people didn't normally desire to leave the band or tribe to which they were accustomed. Prehistoric people most likely couldn't have conceived of any alternative to tribal life.

The relatively small amount of information known about nomadic, prehistoric bands includes the knowledge that their social organization was frequently based on close family ties. I'd affirm that a prehistoric band was not an organization that forced significant interaction between people who'd otherwise not choose each other's company. Members of the band would be relatives or people voluntarily joining together out of a strong mutual interest: survival. Most of their mutual activities would relate to survival. In the interest of convenience and due to our lack of knowledge about prehistoric social structures, it is appropriate to think of prehistoric times as being absent of afriations.

When I was educated, we were taught that the valleys of the Tigris, the Euphrates, and the Nile Rivers were considered "the cradle of civilization." Now it is known that other civilizations independently developed just as early or even earlier in Peru, Mexico, Pakistan, and India. The crux of the matter was that in these areas, people learned to raise grain and livestock and no longer had to migrate for food. Their periodic food surpluses enabled them to trade some of their crops for goods or services. Trade centers grew into villages and villages grew into small cities of merchants, craftsmen, and builders. Social systems that usually included rulers and social castes developed simultaneously. This new phenomenon called "civilization" has existed for only five and one half thousand years.

Throughout the vast majority of civilization's duration, most people lived with no afriats. Small family farmers sometimes had to hire the services of millers, blacksmiths, shoemakers, potters, butchers, bakers, candlestick makers, brick masons, tinkers, metal smiths, and other tradesmen who could be considered occasionals. Most craftsmen, tradesmen, and merchants were self-employed and taught their trades to their sons. Their customers were among their occasionals. Like farmers, they virtually existed without afriats.

This social scenario of small farms, small villages, and independent merchants and craftsmen would probably exist worldwide today if not for the category of people I've labeled effectuals, people whose decisions affect our lives drastically from a distance. In ancient times, of course, effectuals had no media or global economy to help spread their influence. Political, economic, and social control of regions was gained through military conquest. Ancient armies were most likely the world's first afriations.

To enforce his rules and policies, a conqueror or an established ruler needed to display the threat of punishment to his subjects. The simplest form of punishment, of course, was to merely put any dissenters to death. A fate that seems worse than death to many was devised when rulers first conceived of prisons. Ancient prisons were most likely the world's second afriations.

Conquering armies in ancient times were often instructed to capture and bring back conquered people to be forced into servitude. The institution of slavery was probably the world's third type of afriation. Gradual increases in the number of nobility and successful merchants gave rise to the occupation of hired servants, most likely the world's fourth type of afriation. Probably no other form of afriations but these four existed during ancient and medieval civilization.

As long as they stayed out of their effectuals' prisons, armies, and slave galleys, and as long as they took no employment as servants, the vast majority of ancient farmers, craftsmen, tradesmen, and merchants lived their lives with no afriats. This setting continued for thousands of years, even through centuries of the feudal systems of medieval Europe. Let's imagine ourselves for a moment as medieval serfs. Our main effectual would be a king we've heard so much about but perhaps have never seen. His soldiers who'd arrive periodically to collect his taxes and inspect his kingdom would be our occasionals. The feudal landowner who'd come by occasionally to inspect our work and collect his share of our profits would also be an occasional. If our landlord instead sent his servants to do the collecting and inspecting, the landlord would be our effectual rather than our occasional, and the visiting servants would be our occasionals. Small shopkeepers and skilled craftsmen would be among the numerous occasionals with whom we'd interact. If we were independent farmers, we'd likely interact with these occasionals a little more often than we could afford to as serfs.

If we were millers, carpenters, blacksmiths, tailors, shoemakers, masons, bakers, or shopkeepers, we'd have approximately the same types of effectuals and occasionals: the soldiers who collected the king's taxes; the servants who collected the nobility's taxes; the property owner who collected his rent. We'd rely on customers and clients for our income, and at times we'd need to seek the services of other tradesmen. All these people would be among our occasionals.

Which interactional category was lacking in the lives of these peasants and common workers? Afriats. Except for prisoners, soldiers, slaves and servants, only effectuals had afriats, namely the soldiers and servants they relied on to carry out their dictates. With no form of media and no widespread, unified economy, the price one had to pay for being an effectual was being surrounded by afriats. But common workers and agrarians continued to live without afriats until that second great social phenomenon, the Industrial Revolution, was brought on by their effectuals.

A generation after the American Revolution, less than ten percent of Americans and Europeans lived in villages, towns, or cities. Farmers were self-sufficient to a large degree, normally making much of their own clothes, furniture, and tools. What goods and services farmers couldn't acquire through their own ingenuity had to be bought from village merchants and craftsmen. Manufacturing was done by hand in individuals' homes or in small shops.

The Industrial Revolution ignited in England near the dawn of the nineteenth century. A few effectuals developed a few innovations in textile production that quickly led to the first textile factories. The financial success of textile factories soon encouraged effectuals to build factories for producing many other kinds of manufactured goods. Factory production meant machine production, and it proved so cost effective that small-shop manufacturers still working by hand could not compete and were driven out of business. This situation often forced former shopkeepers to work twelve to fourteen hours a day in a factory.

The resulting increase in production gave rise to a new class of wealthy effectuals as the concept of big business was put into practice. The development of major banks and office buildings that employed many people followed. Education, which had historically been available to only the elite, became much more widespread and eventually became mandatory. As rural people relocated into towns to do factory work, crowded apartment dwellings became more and more common. For the first time in history, the general population began to experience life with many afriats.

British authorities tried to confine the Industrial Revolution to England, but by the mid-nineteenth century, it had inevitably spread to the United States and throughout much of Western Europe. By then, the effectuals who invented railroads had created distribution potentials unimagined a few decades earlier. Increased distribution, of course, meant increased marketing outlets, which meant increased production to meet increased demand. The phenomenon became a spiraling, self-feeding cycle, always on the increase. Until recently, industrial societies believed that natural resources were unlimited, that industrial wastes wouldn't harm this planet's air, water, land, plant life, or animal life, and that the answer to most human wants and needs was simply to increase production.

Of course, the spread of industrialism wasn't geographically uniform. Industrial cities were filled with such afriations as factories, marketing outlets, and apartment complexes, but many small farming area towns with no factories or large businesses continued to exist almost as they had done before the advent of the Industrial Revolution. During the first half of the Twentieth Century, most of rural America was still a land of family farms and small, autonomous towns supporting family businesses. This social structure enabled most people to live with few or no afriats. But a third major phenomenon was developing that would accelerate the spread of afriations even more, what has been referred to as "our romance with the automobile."

By the mid-twentieth century, paved highways allowed fast driving, automobiles were finally reliable, and fuel was cheap. Small-town people began to think nothing of driving thirty or forty miles to a larger city to work or to shop. Small-town businesses, unable to compete with the prices of large, corporate outlets in nearby large cities, all but disappeared during the second half of the twentieth century. Former small business owners found themselves commuting to nearby large cities to work in large afriations. Corporately bought and run farms displaced the majority of unafriated farmers throughout the second half of the twentieth century, and caused many of them to seek employment in large urban afriations. By the nineteen sixties, only a very small percent of modern people, perhaps mainly the most capable people, were able to experience unafriated lives.

Of course, another phenomenon that enormously accelerated the widespread expansion of afriations was World War Two. I have always been grateful to the eighteen million Americans in uniform who stopped our despotic foreign effectuals from conquering our nation. I've also been grateful to the American factories whose round-the-clock production enabled our armed forces to win that terrible war. But the demands of war production taught industrial America how to super produce, putting the enormous gears of production into motion. The physical and social repercussions of that war are still enormous, more than six decades later.

I've heard World War Two referred to as "The Great Homogenizer." Standard assembly line production, originally developed in early automobile factories, became manufacturing's norm The everything-looks-the-same era followed the war, and new products, business edifices, housing, neighborhoods and shopping centers all began to look like they were made from the same set of plans. Efficient military-fashioned chain outlets, chain restaurants, chain groceries, and chain service providers of all types throughout postwar America nearly rendered small, unafriated businesses extinct.

It can be fascinating to walk through old neighborhoods built before World War II. Most of them were built for a pedestrian and a horse and buggy population. It's an interesting study to observe among the old houses all the quaint little buildings that until the mid-twentieth century housed small, unafriated businesses. It's interesting to speculate on what kind of a family business the little shops were built to house. Many were corner groceries, some were little bakeries, some were small pharmacies, theatres, shoe shops, livery stables, harness shops, bookstores, barber shops, or cafes, all owned by local citizens and operated by very few people.

Contrast these formerly busy, quaint little business districts to the modern standardized shopping malls that have extinguished them. From a historical point of view, it is astounding and almost incredible that a community can change from a relatively unafriated society to one of almost total afriation in one generation. That's an extremely rapid pace of change for a species that until recently was totally nomadic. As I mentioned earlier, the drastic effects of such rapid, unexpected change were discussed brilliantly in the early nineteen seventies by Alvin Toffler in his book *Future Shock*.

In the past two or three decades, another social-economic phenomenon has greatly affected many kinds of afriations in the United States. American manufacturing companies have been largely moving their plants and factories overseas to countries that until very recently were not at all industrialized. Cheaper labor, lower taxes, fewer environmental mandates, and eased foreign trade agreements have all been factors in this mass migration. The result, of course, has been the near disappearance of the factory-manufacturing segment of our society. America has fast become a market for third-world-manufactured goods. Currently, America's largest and most numerous afriations are within the marketing and the service industries.

In less than one and a half decades, another phenomenon has developed that has already begun to exert a drastic influence on modern afriations. I know less about computerization than any person I've met, but its social-economic implications are obvious. Many marketers, buyers, shippers, and investors are conducting most of their transactions via the Internet, eliminating much of the need for personal interaction and thus eliminating some if not all of their occasionals and afriats. If marketing and shopping via Internet becomes pervasive, we may soon see a major shift away from shopping-mall-styled afriations toward small, unafriated home businesses.

But to my limited knowledge, computers can't raise crops, reap raw materials, manufacture consumer and industrial goods, or deliver products. Even if most retailing goes on line, widespread afriations will persist as long as large-scale, standardized production and distribution persist. Widespread afriation is still a new phenomenon, highly unstable, and always likely to be affected by unpredictable decisions of our effectuals. I can't offer much foresight into its future directions.

12

THE NATURE OF AFRIATIONS

In review, an *afriat* is a person whose company we wouldn't normally choose. We are regularly forced to interact with the afriat by an *afriation*, which is an organization, an institution, or a situation that forces extensive, involuntary interaction.

Some people initially object to categorizing work associates as afriats. They argue, "You chose to accept work in that jobsite. You can quit and look for another job if you're not satisfied. Nobody is forcing you to be there; therefore nothing is forcing you to interact with these people. That means they aren't afriats."

Of course, there have been despotic governments that have dictated people's occupations and worksites, as recently as cold war Russia, China, and Cuba, to say nothing of the World War II Axis powers. But granted, in most comparatively free societies, citizens aren't officially ordered to work in a specific location. However, government effectuals or single-contact influentials are not the only entities that can force people into a particular employment situation. Our economic necessities, our particular talents or lack of jobs skills, job availability, and the unavailability of self-employment opportunities are all factors that collectively dictate where we make our living.

Think of any company where you've ever worked. Would any of the managers or workers be there day after day if they didn't feel they had to be? Of course, if they feel dissatisfied, they are free to resign and seek employment elsewhere, but likely they'd find no other options than to take a similar position in a similar afriation and face similar dissatisfactions. Most people simply don't have much choice when it comes to accepting or rejecting an afriation of employment.

But it is not the element of coercion that determines whether or not an organization is an afriation. It's determined simply by the fact that it regularly forces undesired interpersonal interactions. For our purposes, even a voluntary social organization can be considered an afriation if it causes frequent interactions between unlikely parties. Fraternal organizations such as college fraternities and sororities, or middle-aged people's lodges named after animals are handy examples of common social afriations.

Now I can imagine hearing some lodge members interjecting, "Hold it. These are my friends, not afriats. This is a brotherhood, you know."

True, probably the majority of fraternal lodge members joined because they have one or more friends in the order. Some people join because they are attracted by certain activities. Others join out of loneliness, having insufficient interests and activities to attract true friends. It's easy to think of all club members as friends or brothers in an organization that is essentially recreational or social. But at the core of any social organization are the people responsible for making its decisions. Friction between individual office holders or committee members commonly emerges. Political rivalry between different circles of friends is seen more commonly in social afriations that in afriations of employment.

Within most social organizations, certainly we are likely to have some friends, but we can also expect to frequently be in the company of afriats and occasionals. The distinction between pleasant afriats and friends isn't always clear in recreational organizations, especially when people are sharing enjoyable activities. In determining whether members of a social organization are our friends or our afriats, each member needs to be examined individually. The litmus test is this: "If this organization ceased to exist, would this member and I voluntarily seek each other's company to share common interests, activities, or affections?" If the answer is honestly "yes," consider that member a friend. If the answer is a definite "no," the member is an afriat. If the answer is "maybe," "I don't know," or even "I'd hope so," consider that member a fond occasional or a pleasant afriat, but not a true friend.

Other social organizations that could be considered afriations include business clubs, chambers of commerce, church organizations, youth recreational clubs, athletic teams, civic clubs, veterans' clubs, physical fitness clubs, bars, unions, and employee organizations. Because there is no economic necessity for anyone to remain a member, they are much easier to quit or to do without in the first place than afriations of employment. For that reason, most of the discussions and suggestions in this book will pertain to afriations of employment.

This is still an untested theory, but my observations have led me to believe that the majority of people in contemporary American society interact more with afriats than with members of any of the other six interactional categories, except perhaps for members of their immediate family. However, some people interact with afriats more than with family members. Many people interact with afriats more than with members of all the other interactional categories combined. Of course, there are people who have no afriats, but there are also people in our society whose interpersonal interactions include almost no one but afriats.

The fact that no word has existed until now for the concept of afriation shows how little modern man has contemplated or even recognized this extremely widespread phenomenon. Initially, I found that surprising; now I find it almost incredible. Of course, people in "undeveloped countries" with no industry or mandatory education would lack such a term, for they would lack such a concept. But why a term for *afriation* has been lacking until now in the industrialized world is hard to fathom. The only likely explanation is that we are institutionally conditioned as children to take afriations for granted and to accept them as normal and natural.

Historically speaking, widespread afriation is still relatively new. When the Industrial Revolution became widespread, it was soon followed by widespread education. Today, most preschool aged children have two parents who work or, in many cases, a single parent who is employed. Preschools, referred to in my youth as "nursery schools," and infantile day care centers are most children's first afriations. Here they begin to learn society's concepts of appropriate behavior toward afriats: "Don't hit or push them; don't take toys away from them; don't yell at them or say unkind things to them; share your toys with them and play with them nicely; learn to like everybody and remember, we're all friends here."

Of course, some of these instructions are important social lessons for children to learn. But unfortunately, it marks the beginning of people's inability to recognize an afriation and to distinguish afriats from friends. Small children find themselves in an institution where they may not want to be, but they are taught they belong in this institution until their parents are free to leave their required institutions and take them home. They are regularly put in the company of other preschoolers, some of whom they'd choose as playmates but others whom they wouldn't choose. They are instructed to be "friends" with all their preschool afriats, something noble indeed in principle but seldom possible, and told they are "bad" if they can't befriend everybody present. The result is that years later, in afriations of employment, they fail to distinguish afriats from friends, and that mistake can be costly, as we'll discuss in the next chapter.

If a young child misses the day care and preschool experience—perhaps the child has one parent who isn't employed or the child is left with a grandparent or a baby sitter—the same conditioning awaits for him or her in mandatory kindergartens, classes that used to convene for only a few hours, but now are normally scheduled for the entire school day. Today kindergartens seem to undertake a little more academic instruction than they did when I was a child, but still their main role is "socialization," a term applied to the process of teaching children to fit into an afriation. After kindergarten, academics become an increasingly larger part of the child's curriculum, but training in socialization continues throughout grade school.

I well recall attending grade school during the first post-war decade. Four times a year we were issued a large, folded, stiff-papered report card that opened at the fold like a large birthday card. On the left side of the fold were the grades for all the academics such as spelling, writing, arithmetic, grammar, art, music, reading, history, geography, and penmanship. On the right side of the fold were grades for what the school system termed "citizenship." This consisted entirely of social attributes such as: Does the student follow directions? Does the student play well with others? Does the student listen to the teacher? Does the student maintain a pleasant attitude? Does the student cooperate? Does the student appear neat and clean? Does the student use a handkerchief?

Perhaps these are important social skills to acquire to enable a youth to function in an afriation. But a by-product of our childhood training is that we have long been conditioned to taking afriations for granted, even to the point that our language lacks a word for the concept. By the time a youngster finishes school, he or she can hardly fathom an existence without afriats, any more than a nomad could have imagined existing with them.

As a result of childhood conditioning, people enter afriations of employment unaware of the concept of afriats and of the other six interactional categories. People new to a work afriation tend to mentally classify everyone present in terms of which employees are managers and which are workers. First they consider the managers, needing to find out what these people expect and how to make a favorable impression on them in the interest of keeping the job and eventually being promoted. Someone new to an afriation but quite experienced in similar afriations will try to quickly learn about the managers' supervisional practices in order to know when to appear productive and when it's safe to "goof off."

The person new to the afriation can then turn his or her attention to the co-workers. A person with sufficient experience in workplace afriations is more likely to approach the new afriats more cautiously. A person relatively new to the experience is more likely to clumsily barge into the social order. Conditioned by childhood education to think of afriats as friends, and having been told by the interviewing personnel manager "we are a team," the inexperienced afriat is likely to initially approach every other afriat as a "friend." He'll find this approach works well enough with a fraction of the co-workers. Others will react courteously but will remain cautiously neutral.

Still others are likely to respond coldly, perhaps somewhat resenting this premature showing of friendliness on behalf of the newcomer.

Within most modern work afriations, newcomers usually face what I refer to as the *ritual of scrutiny*. Initially, many afriats will knowingly or subliminally try to keep some distance, physical or personal, between themselves and a new arrival to the afriation. Their scrutiny will eventually determine if the new afriat is going to "work out" in the workplace or will sooner or later be "let go." Many afriats fear it could be detrimental to their job standing to have any managers associate them with a new employee who may prove unsuitable for the position and be dismissed. Others fear it may be undesirable to be associated with a new employee who for whatever reason may prove unpopular with his or her co-afriats. When joining an afriation, we should always expect to be subjected to this ritual of scrutiny until reluctant afriats feel comfortable that we as newcomers are not a personal liability.

People inexperienced with afriations may not expect this cold scrutiny. Conditioned as children to believe that everyone in the afriation should be "friends," they often take this initial distancing for the purpose of scrutiny as a blatant rejection of friendship. Unfamiliar with the concept of afriats, they've been conditioned to look at everyone as either "friend or foe." Too frequently, the new arrival will respond to this perceived coldness with his or her own style of coldness or rudeness that will in turn aggravate the scrutinizing afriat. The normal result is that subtle hostilities reciprocally develop and spiral into the kind of relationships that commonly make a workplace miserable.

This common type of afriat infighting can often be avoided if the new arrival anticipates and is willing to succumb to the ritual of scrutiny. Whether we like it or not, it's part of the nature of afriations. Things will go much smoother in the long run if we simply let the reluctant afriats take whatever time they feel they need to scrutinize us. Don't rush them. The less secure they feel within the afriation, the longer it will likely take them to scrutinize us.

I believe that when entering a new afriation of employment, it is wise to initially think of everyone in the workplace as an afriat. (In a coming chapter, I will discuss behavior appropriate to that concept.) Soon it will become more apparent which employees are occasionals, not afriats. Remember, occasionals are distinguished from afriats in that our interactions with them are more limited. Within our new afriation, we may discover some afriats with interests or activities that match ours, and some friendships may emerge. That can happen gradually or quickly. Once we befriend an afriat, of course, we need to mentally recategorize him or her as a friend, even if we continue to work with him or her in the same afriation.

In discussing the nature of afriations, it is important to recognize and remember a concept that I will remind you of a few times in the ensuing chapters: *Afriations in themselves cannot produce friendships.* They can and commonly do expose us to people we befriend, but the causes of these new friendships are the common interests, activities, or affections shared, not the afriations themselves. The assumption that someone is our "friend" simply because "we work together" is a fallacy that can lead to the problems we'll discuss in the next chapter.

I know two elderly gentlemen who worked together in a smelter for thirty-four years. Although they were comfortable working together, they never once associated with each other outside of work. They simply had no common interests or activities to cause a true friendship. Today, after years of retirement, they get together regularly to have a drink or some lunch and to reminisce. On the surface, cases like this could lead us to conclude that perhaps afriations can cause friendships. But in actuality, it is not the afriation but a common interest that unites and befriends them: their interest in reminiscing about past experiences in a common workplace. Common interests, activities, and affections are what produce friendships, not afriations.

In large afriations of employment, of course, we can expect to find people of varied ethnicity, backgrounds, age groups, creeds, activities, and values. We can dismiss these differences as being irrelevant to our consideration of forced interactions. I find it handy to think of most afriats as fitting into one of three subcategories. Like many of the systems of classification I've listed, this one may seem like an over simplification, but it provides a handy terminology for referring to the nature of our most commonly-encountered afriats.

The first subcategory of afriats can simply be thought of as our *positive afriats*. These are the afriats that strike us as being the most friendly, pleasant, cooperative, and helpful. They often seem to like us and we tend to like them, so of course we tend to "buddy up" with *positive afriats* while on duty in the afriation. Of course, it is the afriats of this subcategory who are most likely to emerge as our friends, but it is sometimes easy to regard them as friends prematurely. This misjudgment can often lead to problems, as we'll discuss in the next chapter.

The litmus test to distinguish between friends and positive afriats in an afriation of employment is the same test we utilized in categorizing members of a social afriation: "If the afriation that binds us were no longer to exist, would we still seek each other's company to share mutual interests, activities, or affections?"

If the answer is "yes," of course, we should recategorize them as friends. Otherwise they are to be thought of as positive afriats, which, of course, is still a highly desirable relationship.

The second subcategory of afriats I've labeled *neutral afriats*. As this title suggests, their perceived attitude toward us seems neither complimentary nor derogatory. Their behavior toward us seems neither cordial nor hostile. They seem neither friendly nor unfriendly, neither helpful nor unhelpful, neither cooperative nor uncooperative, neither pleasant nor unpleasant, neither interested nor uninterested. They typically try to minimize required interactions and seem to radiate the message, "I'm here to do my job. Don't bother me and I won't bother you." It's usually best to heed and respect that message and never become their pidoca.

The third subcategory of afriats can be considered *negative afriats*. Their disposition toward us ranges from indifferent to unfriendly. Their behavior toward us ranges from coldly uncomfortable to verbally hostile. Sometimes they are our supervisors. If not, they typically have been in the afriation longer than we have and tend to think of their longevity and experience as factors that give them authority over us. Negative afriats frequently seem dissatisfied with our performance or our demeanor. They often voice complaints about us and occasionally threaten to have us dismissed from the afriation. Of course, they sometimes carry out those threats.

Negative afriats can't always define their dislike for us. Most of us at one time or another experience an uneasy dislike for certain people, or at least we feel uncomfortable in their presence, without understanding the cause of our distaste. Some people try to explain this phenomenon as a "chemical" incompatibility. Some people call it a difference in "karma." Some people consider it an electrical-magnetic opposition that they refer to as "bad vibes." In the next chapter when we discuss this phenomenon in more detail, I will refer to it as *the phenomenon of irrational repulsion*. It simply hasn't been explained yet by modern science or modern psychology. At any rate, almost everyone feels this incompatibility with someone from time to time.

When an unexplainable incompatibility is sensed between two people, the natural thing to do is to go separate ways and to categorize one another as irrelevants. Of course, being afriated to each other makes that impossible. I'll have some suggestions as to how to interact with negative afriats in Chapter Fourteen. What most commonly happens is the newer arrival to the afriation quickly resents the negative afriat's demeanor and begins to reciprocate with his or her personal style of unfriendliness, uncooperativeness, rudeness, and passive hostility. The negative affriate, sensing this behavior to be insubordination or excessive offensiveness, typically resorts to more aggressive tactics. He or she may try to have the new afriat fired from the afriation, or may try to harass the new afriat into resigning.

Aggravated afriats is a convenient term to use when referring to negative afriats who become temperamental and/or aggressive toward us. In cases like this, neither the aggravated afriat nor the victim is familiar with the concept of an afriat. Preconditioned to look at people as either "friend or foe," they mistake each other for enemies and allow the conflict to escalate until one of the afriats—usually the newer of the two—is transferred or terminated.

When we talk about afriational problems more in detail, it will always be necessary to distinguish between the category enemies and the subcategory negative afriats. You will recall I earlier defined an enemy as someone who would willfully and knowingly harm us, our friends, or our property. Essentially the same litmus test that we used to distinguish between positive afriats and friends applies here. We need to ask ourselves, "If the afriation were to disappear, would this aggravated afriat still be trying to do me harm?" In the vast majority of cases, the answer will be "no," meaning the person in question is not our enemy. If it weren't for the afriation, the person in question would simply be an irrelevant.

On rare occasions, the answer to that question is "yes." In such cases, our enemy's motive is almost always revenge. A fired afriat may seek to avenge a former afriat who he feels caused him or her an unjust fate. An expelled middle school student might want to beat up—or in this day and age, shoot—a former afriat who informed on him. Aggravated afriats can and too often do become true enemies. At this point, of course, we should no longer classify them as afriats.

Earlier in this chapter, I suggested that afriations in themselves are not able to produce friends. On the other hand, they can and often do produce enemies. The most extreme cases all too frequently appear in national headlines, regular accounts of afriats, most often students or employees, who become furious at members of their afriations and storm in with a gun to take the lives of as many afriats as possible. These aggravated afriats are normally dismissed as "disturbed." Of course they are disturbed, badly enough to want to take the lives of others and usually their own. The question that needs more attention is, "Is there something about the nature of afriations that might cause certain kinds of afriats to become so violently disturbed?"

Fortunately, most enemies that emerge from afriations are neither as violent nor as disturbed as the examples I just mentioned. Fortunately also, making enemies of negative afriats could almost always be avoided, but it would require that the public shed its "friend or foe" mentality. This process must begin in early childhood.

I have worked in dozens of afriations throughout my varied life, doing everything from physical labor to afriational supervision. One year I worked in a public school system's after-school childcare program. One of the most common complaints I would hear from cute little tattlers was, "Johnny said he's not my friend."

What I wished I could say to all those rejected little folks was, "That's okay. He doesn't have to be your friend. If he just wants to be an afriat, let him be an afriat. Don't aggravate him." Of course, the child wouldn't understand that explanation, so I'd normally answer, "That's his problem. We don't have to worry about that." The child would almost always seem surprised at not hearing me warn, "Johnny, you'd *better* be Suzy's friend." This unnatural expectation that everybody in our afriation is obligated to be our "friend," universally drilled into children in grade school, remains a major part of our conditioning well into adulthood, often manifesting itself in the "friend or foe" mentality that can make an afriation a living hell.

Instead of teaching early school children to expect every other child in the afriation to be their friend, why not teach them that there are indeed seven interactional categories of human beings and one of the categories is that of afriats? Teach them that within most afriations, we should expect to encounter some neutral and even a few negative afriats, and that attempts to quickly befriend them can sometimes aggravate them. Teach them the suggestions that I will present in Chapter Fourteen about how to interact with unfavorable afriats. Teach them above all not to mistake negative afriats for enemies.

With the benefit of such instruction, the public would possess the vocabulary and the concepts needed to analyze difficult afriational situations. I believe that many of our afriational conflicts would then be avoided. Fewer aggravated afriats would engage in low-profile but long-term struggles in which "passive aggressiveness" is the main weapon. Most likely, fewer aggravated afriats would resort to high-profile tactics, such as returning to the afriation with a gun or a bomb.

When discussing the nature of afriations, the terms "positive," "neutral," and "negative" prove to be handy. But always remember that membership in these subcategories is not etched in stone. Afriats can be ambivalent, endlessly shifting from one subcategory to another. Perhaps the most common examples are afriats whom we initially perceive as neutral who later become positive afriats, a process that often accompanies the ritual of scrutiny. The positive afriat could sooner or later become a pidoca, or we ourselves could become the pidoca, making the afriat our aspirat. Sometimes a neutral afriat conducts the ritual of scrutiny and decides to consider us negative afriats, not because we are unfriendly or unpleasant, but because our opinions about procedures don't dovetail with his or hers. The afriat's reaction toward us, of course, will cause us to mentally recategorize him or her as a negative afriat.

In most large afriations, we will find a few afriats who switch from subcategory to subcategory extremely quickly, frequently, and unpredictably. The other afriats often describe him or her with such phrases as "he runs hot and cold" or "you never know which way she's gonna' turn." Such ambivalent afriats are often in positions of authority. The classic example is the boss who's patting us on the back and praising us one minute and blowing up over our mistakes the next. These afriats are as hard to categorize as they are to predict. For lack of a better term, I refer to them as *hot-and-cold afriats.* I personally find them the hardest afriats to endure. I prefer the company of an afriat whose temperament is always volatile to one whose volatility can never be predicted.

Remember, these three subcategories of afriats are based on the perception of each of us individually. In other words, the classification is in the eye of the beholder. We can perceive an afriat as neutral or negative while another afriat may perceive him or her as positive. Indeed, sometimes afriats are institutionally required to interact positively toward some afriats, neutrally toward others, and negatively toward a few others. That's not to be construed as being devious or "two-faced." It's merely the nature of afriations.

13

THE HARMS OF AFRIATIONS

"So what's the big problem?" I'm sometimes asked when discussing the concept of afriations. "So what if you have to be subjected to the company of some people with whom you otherwise wouldn't associate? Don't you like people? What are you, antisocial or something?"

Such questions always serve to remind me of a point that needs to be acknowledged before discussing the harms of afriations: not everyone seems to be bothered by them. Perhaps the best place to observe this phenomenon is in society's jails.

Once, as a youth, I pleaded guilty to a misdemeanor. The judge offered me a choice between a harsh fine or two weeks in jail. Inspired by the incarceration of late civil disobedience martyrs like Henry David Thoreau, Mahatma Gandhi, and Dr. Martin Luther King, I chose jail. I naively thought I'd use those two quiet weeks to get a lot of rest, catch up on my reading, and perhaps do a little writing. It was undoubtedly my exposure to the postwar media that had given me the impression that jail cells are places where you can accomplish such things.

I quickly learned that jail cells are almost always overcrowded. The one I occupied was approximately fourteen feet by six feet and housed eight afriats. Eight cells of this size opened into a small television and smoking lounge called a "dayroom." Sixty-four chain-smoking afriats would spill into this room during most of the hours when we weren't "locked down." This was the most intensive spell of afriation I've ever experienced.

I realized then that what makes jail time so terrible to many people is not the element of confinement itself, but the intensively crowded afriation that accompanies it. Some people find it complete mental torture and quickly develop mental illness. I cannot document this, but my limited jail experience has convinced me that many of the suicides that take place in jails are committed by people who can't tolerate intense afriations.

Yet as I acknowledged earlier, some people seem oblivious to afriations. In every overcrowded jail cell, there are usually one or two afriats who seem content with their plight. Indeed, many chronic jail dwellers seem to thrive on it. They usually spend about an equal amount of time in and out of jail. They are often homeless, but many own homes or rent apartments. What they almost always lack are activities and interests that they would dread to miss during incarceration. Most often they seem to have no real friends in life and they likely become lonely when they are out of jail.

Afriats of this nature seem glad to be back in jail, perceiving it as their best opportunity for interpersonal interactions. They are the kind of afriats that the more reticent inmates say are "always in your face." They lack the concepts of afriation and bring to the jail their "friend or foe" mentality. They can become dangerous because they tend to consider their afriats who reject them to be their enemies.

Evidence that some people are not troubled much by afriations is also apparent in most large afriations of employment. These unaffected people seem to fall into two categories. One category consists of some very well-adjusted, balanced individuals. These people usually have numerous friends and most often a family life, and a variety of activities and interests. They know how to utilize the practices that minimize afriational stress that we will discuss in the next chapter. I think of these individuals as our *balanced afriats*.

The other category somewhat resembles its counterpart in jails. Outside of the afriation of employment, these afriats have few if any interests or activities to share with others, and therefore have few if any true friends. Unfamiliar with the concept of afriats and the principle that afriations themselves can't cause friendships, they commonly mistake their afriats for friends. They become known for always giving cheap Christmas gifts to all their afriats or repeatedly trying to organize afriational social events.

This in itself seems harmless and even "nice of them," and it isn't a big problem as long as these afriats don't make pidocas of themselves. Unfortunately, that's exactly what they often do. Like their counterparts in jails, they perceive their afriation of employment to be an institution of friendship and think of everyone as either "friend or foe." They are often quick to think that anyone who declines their efforts toward friendship is an enemy, causing them to initiate subtle antagonisms. In my observation, the majority of interpersonal conflicts in afriations begin with this unrealistic expectation of being treated as a friend by all our afriats. I'd suspect that many of the shootings in afriations of education or employment also have roots in this "friend or foe" mentality.

Yes, some people don't seem to mind being heavily afriated, while others feel it drives them insane. Most of us fit somewhere between those two extremes. It's easy to discern the generally disgruntled temperament in regard to afriations that is so highly pervasive throughout our working population.

If you're like me, you find that "overhearing" conversations in public places can often be quite educational. Tell me, what's the most commonly complained about topic of the conversations you overhear? On first thought, you might be tempted to answer, "Our effectuals, people like the president, the governor, and other politicians, plus the effectuals who control the prices and availability of goods and who continually redesign today's torrent of technology." True, a lot of grumbling about effectuals can commonly be overheard. I'd say the topic of effectuals is probably the second most commonly complained about subject of the conversations I overhear.

I have no doubt that the most commonly complained about subject of conversation I overhear is that of afriats. Just listen to people wherever you go: "… that jerk I have for a foreman …"; "… those clowns I've got working for me …"; "… those idiots I work with …"; "… my mean, ugly old teacher …"; "… my spoiled, lazy students …"; "… those nerds in my science class …"; "… our rude, noisy, inconsiderate neighbors …"; "… that big liar in our car pool …"; "… my husband's nosey sister …"; "… my wife's pesky parents …"; "… those ungrateful complainers I care for at the assisted living center …"; "… the slave driver we have for a platoon sergeant …"; "… that drunk across the hall …" Afriats, afriats, afriats.

Throughout our lives, most of us seem to have more problems with afriats than with members of all the other six interactional categories combined. Of course, there are extreme cases that prove to be exceptions to this trend. An enemy who hurts us badly enough to disable us for life certainly does us more damage than all our afriats. An effectual who declares our religious or political beliefs to be unlawful and imprisons us certainly does us more damage than our afriats. But most often, enemies or effectuals do us an abrupt but short-term harm that we can overcome, learn from, and go beyond. Negative afriats, on the other hand, tend to gnaw away at us slowly but steadily, causing a misery that we seemingly can't shed as long as we are members of the afriation.

The harms of afriations are hard to document for two reasons. The first reason, of course, is that the concept of this phenomenon has gone unrecognized to the extent that no name has been applied to it until now. No controlled research or surveys have been conducted that pertain specifically to afriations. If I were thirty years younger, I would begin to conduct such research myself, but I don't expect to be dwelling on this planet long enough to accomplish a lengthy research project. As I mentioned earlier, most of my ideas are based on long-term, personal observation as opposed to scientific research. People have every right to look upon these concepts as unproven, philosophical theories.

The second reason the harms of afriations are hard to substantiate is that as of yet neither modern science nor modern psychology has been able to explain *the phenomenon of irrational repulsion*. As I mentioned earlier, a feeling of interpersonal repulsion frequently exists between two individuals that is beyond our current understanding. Today it's easy for people to reject any belief that can't be scientifically verified. Yet there are many phenomena in our universe that science can't logically explain. At any rate, our daily language is heavily laced with expressions that indicate people recognize and believe in the phenomenon of irrational repulsion. A few examples are: "I'm uncomfortable around him." "I get a bad feeling from her." "He rubs me the wrong way." "We don't click." "He gets under my skin." "She gives me the creeps." "I clash with that guy." "We don't hit it off." "He has bad vibes." "Our chemistry just doesn't mix." "We don't jell." "I detect bad energy from her." "I've been picking up on his bad karma." "We don't jive." "We are incompatible." "He gives me the willies."

It is natural for us to avoid people we feel very uncomfortable around and to categorize them as irrelevants. However, if we are afriated to them, then of course we are not free to disassociate from them. Although I am not aware of any research that has been conducted concerning the phenomenon of irrational repulsion, I believe most of us have experienced it and many of us have been subjected to considerable stress on account of it. I need to rely on an assumed validity of this phenomenon to maintain that afriations produce harmful effects on our mental, emotional, and physical well-being.

Although no research has been conducted concerning afriational stress in particular, an internet search of "causes of stress in the workplace" can bring forth a large number of studies that repeatedly illustrate two important concepts: first, that workplace-related stress is highly pervasive throughout modern society, and secondly, that afriats are either the leading cause of workplace stress or are at least among the leading causes. The studies I am about to cite to illustrate these two points represent only a tiny fraction of the findings available. I'd encourage any reader to investigate other similar studies. Before I mention a few findings, let's quickly review the nature of stress and its effect on human beings.

In simple terms, stress can be defined as a state of physical and/or mental tension produced by a perceived threat to our well-being. The threat may be very real or it may be imagined. Either way, it activates what is commonly referred to as our "fight or flight mechanism." Our hormones, our nervous systems, our muscles, our cardiovascular systems, and our respiratory systems quickly become prepared for a physical reaction to our perceived adversity. Stress, of course, is not a disease in itself, but its continual presence significantly increases wear and tear on our biological systems as it renders the human body unable to adequately defend and repair itself. It can lead to a wide variety of mental and physical health disorders.

As I've mentioned, I am not a doctor, but information about stress-related maladies is widely accessible to the public. Some of the health disorders that stress can cause or at least contribute to are: headache; neck ache; backache; neck, shoulder, and arm cramps; poor memory; poor concentration; irritability; anger; tiredness; apathy; poor bowel movements; disorders of the digestive system; chest pains; excessive sleepiness; sex problems; alcohol and drug abuse; ulcers; asthma; psoriasis; heart disease; diabetes; suppression of the part of the immune system involved in fighting cancer; and depression.

While I am mentioning depression, let me briefly refer to a very recent (October, 2007) national survey conducted by the Federal Substance Abuse and Mental Health Services Administration. The survey determined that seven percent of America's full-time workers experienced serious depression during the past year. By "serious," they mean a spell of depression lasting two weeks or more. As I read some of the percentages for specific occupations, I noticed that the percentages are considerably higher for highly afriated occupations and noticeably lower for less afriated occupations. For example, 10.3% of the workers in the food and beverage industry, such as bartenders, waiters, waitresses, and cooks, suffered from two or more weeks of depression. 11% of personal care workers, including people who care for children, the elderly, and the disabled, witnessed serious depression. These are all jobs that involve a high degree of afriation. On the other hand, only 4.3% of architects, engineers, and surveyors experienced serious depression. These professions usually involve a considerably lower degree of afriation.

Of course, stress in life is often caused by matters other than the workplace. However, surveys conducted by both Yale and Princeton Universities conclude that work-related stress leads to far more health problems than stress from any of the other leading causes, including financial matters, family matters, or personal matters. The European Agency for Safety and Health at Work computes that more than half of employee absenteeism in the United States is due to work-related stress. The American Institute of Stress estimates that job stress costs American industry three hundred billion dollars a year. A Gallop Poll conducted in 2001 concluded that eighty percent of American Workers feel stressed on the job, and a Yale University survey adds that twenty-nine percent of our workers say they are "extremely stressed." The evidence is endless that job stress is an extremely pervasive personal and social problem.

Of course, there are factors other than afriats that cause workplace stress. Other causes listed by BUPA, The personal Health Service, include poor working conditions, an overly large work load, the pressure of deadlines, job insecurity, feeling undervalued as an employee, and task difficulty. But the BUPA adds that two of the most common causes of workplace stress are "poor relationships with colleagues" and "an unsupportive boss," in other words, typical afriational difficulties. The United Kingdom's National Work Stress Network also lists "prolonged conflict between individuals" as one of the main causes of workplace induced stress.

In 2004, TSSA Health and Safety Representatives conducted a survey in which 49% of the 211 people questioned claimed they suffered from work-related stress. 85% of those stress sufferers claimed they were experiencing "poor management consultation." 44% of them claimed they were experiencing "poor relationships with colleagues." 41% of the stressed people even claimed to be the victims of "bullying."

The United Kingdom's National Work Stress Network defines "bullying" as intimidating, insulting, belittling, or malicious behavior toward someone in the workplace. It discusses the interesting research and findings of British Professor Carey Cooper during the 1990's. Bullying in the workplace has been shown to cause anxiety, fear, humiliation, frustration, anger, loss of self confidence and self esteem, loss of motivation and productivity and, of course, stress, which often leads to illness and absenteeism. Professor Carey estimates that 40 million workdays are lost a year in the United Kingdom alone due to bullying in the workplace. Bullying's annual cost to the economy of the United Kingdom is between three and four billion pounds per year.

The afriats that Professor Carey considers workplace "bullies" are essentially what I have termed *aggravated negative afriats*. The widespread extent of this phenomenon is well documented by his statistics. What's missing is a disclosure of what motivates an afriat to behave as a "bully." I am unaware of any scientifically conducted study that has attempted to determine such motivation. I can only make speculations based on my thirty years of observing and interpreting afriats' behavior.

I would suppose that a small percent of this bullying is simply the result of a streak of sadism in the "bullies." I am certainly not qualified to discuss whatever the psychological factors are that lead to sadistic behavior. I must suffice it to say I've occasionally known people who just seem to enjoy being cruel. As children, they enjoyed tormenting pets and picking on the neighbor kids, and as adults, they enjoy tormenting workplace afriats. We've all met a few of these "bullies," and it's a dreadful experience being afriated to them. Fortunately, the large majority of aggravated afriats are not these sadists.

I suppose another small percent of this "bullying" is due to a mixture of jealousy and fear. Occasionally an afriat in the workplace will be jealous of a newer afriat's ability, success, or approval, and will fear that the newer afriat will outshine him or her, be promoted over him or her, or perhaps even replace him or her. The jealous, fearful afriat may then attempt to antagonize the newer afriat into resigning or at least performing less effectively. I've seen this occur in a number of afriations and I've been on the receiving end of it more than once. Fortunately, this is not one of the most common reasons afriats become offensive.

I believe that the large majority of conflicts in afriations of employment result from the nature of afriations themselves and from people's widespread lack of understanding them. Of course, afriations vary. The owner of a smaller business who carefully handpicks seven or eight employees has a fairly good chance of developing a relatively compatible staff. A fortunate employee would likely find him or herself afriated to positive afriats, a few of whom he or she may eventually reclassify as friends. People who claim to like their jobs and especially their work colleagues are usually among the lucky afriats who have a favorable afriation.

More typical in today's economy are the larger afriations with a higher rate of turnover. The hiring is done by a personnel manager who is required to be more preoccupied with keeping positions filled than with accruing a staff of afriats who are compatible with one another. When a large selection of people from varied backgrounds, life styles, religious, social, and political beliefs become afriated to each other, a considerable amount of incompatibility is inevitable.

Often this incompatibility is due to causes that are recognizable. Afriats often dislike each other for their political differences, especially when the conflicting beliefs involve a current war or issues of ecology. People are quick to distrust afriats of opposing political parties or of radically different religions. Racial discrimination, although legally banned in afriations of employment, still lives in the hearts of too many people. A strong distrust of people from certain nationalities or ethnic backgrounds has always existed in American society. Today, a national preoccupation with illegal aliens and suicidal terrorists further intensifies feelings of distrust toward certain minorities.

Of course, afriats can and often do dislike other afriats for non-ethnic reasons. They may simply disapprove of a co-afriat's personality traits. The new fads of grooming and dressing adopted by younger generations have always annoyed some members of their parents' generation. Indeed, members of a given generation often experience friction with some of their contemporaries over differences in dress and hairstyle. There seems to be no limit to the causes of distrust and resentment among human beings.

But interpersonal incompatibility may be due to causes that are unrecognizable. When a random selection of people from varied backgrounds are brought together in a large afriation of employment, it's inevitable that the *phenomenon of irrational repulsion* will occur between certain individuals. This is a situation, you will recall, in which we feel repelled by certain people for reasons that aren't apparent, that uncomfortable incompatibility that people dismiss as "bad energy" or "the wrong chemistry."

As I've admitted, I'm no professional psychologist, but I sometimes reflect on a fundamental experiment many of us should recall from our college psychology classes. If mice are forced to live together under more crowded conditions than they would naturally choose, the stress eventually causes the mice to become neurotic. This led some psychologists to suspect that perhaps modern urban dwellers develop a neurosis from their unnatural, overcrowded environments. In a similar manner, I believe that being afriated to people who unexplainably repel us produces a similar stress, if not a neurosis, in the afriats involved.

The danger in this situation is that an affected afriat can and often does mistake the person who irrationally repels him or her for an enemy. With an awareness of the seven interactional categories and the nature of afriations, a logical analysis of the situation would be to tell ourselves, "Now look, this is an afriation, after all, an unnatural, man-made phenomenon that was probably a social mistake as far as mental health is concerned. Just remember, this person is my afriat, not my enemy. If it weren't for the afriation, we would be each other's irrelevants, not enemies." Then we could begin to interact with the afriat according to the principles I will discuss in the next chapter. Instead, people too often enter an afriation with the "friend or foe" mentality that perpetuates and augments common antagonisms between afriats.

The attitude that "we're friends because we work together" is built upon the fallacy that an afriation can cause friendship. As I've mentioned earlier, this is conditioned into us in early childhood, especially in primary school classrooms where children are instructed to look upon all their classmates as "friends," a highly unrealistic possibility indeed. Instead of being taught, "We are all friends because we are in the same classroom," children need to be told, "Some of the children in this class will be your friends because you share some interests and activities. Some of the children here will be your afriats, not because you don't like each other, but simply because you don't have any interests in common. But always be kind and polite to your afriats because they are as good as you and your friends. Someday they may become your friends, but for now, don't be surprised or unhappy if they don't want to play with you." If this attitude were taught to school children, I believe that when they become adults, they would enter an afriation of employment with a more realistic view on how to accept afriats and a lot of resentment and antagonism would be eliminated.

Within every large afriation of employment that I have observed, there are invariably some afriats who mistake their afriats for friends. These afriats commonly don't have much of a social life outside of the afriation, and typically lack the interests and activities to attract many true friends. These are the employees who expect all their afriats to go out for drinks together after work every payday, or to join the company dart team, or to participate in the football pool. Sometimes we may halfheartedly accompany them just to seem "sociable." Other times we may stop and realize that these well-intended folks are afriats, not friends, because of our lack of common interests, and that our time would be more constructively spent pursuing interests that we share with friends rather than trying to entertain afriats with whom we have little in common.

Unfortunately, too many afriats, conditioned by this "friend or foe" mentality, may consider our unwillingness to participate as a rejection of friendship and subliminally feel offended. This can often result in some of our afriats ostracizing us for our "antisocial" behavior, and a few might even adopt the tactics of workplace "bullies." The motive for bullying in such cases is clearly one of revenge. A high degree of conformity is usually expected within afriations, and those who "hear a different drummer" are often persecuted for it.

As I previously mentioned, within any large afriation, we can expect to encounter some positive afriats, some neutral afriats, and some negative afriates. Persons new to an afriation of employment who soon encounter a negative afriat would be wise to analyze the situation as follows: "This person is my afriat, not my enemy. If it weren't for the afriation, we'd simply be irrelevants." Then the new afriat would be mentally prepared to react to the negative afriat in the ways suggested in the next chapter. Too often a new afriat, conditioned to accept the "friend or foe" fallacy, will be quick to consider a negative afriat or even a neutral afriat conducting the ritual of scrutiny to be an enemy and react with passive aggression or even open hostility. The negative afriat is then likely to counteract with tactics that the new afriat might construe as "bullying." It's a vicious cycle that could be avoided if the afriats involved understood the nature of afriations.

Occasionally, even our positive afriats can be the source of afriational tension. It's easy to think of a positive afriat as a "friend" when interactions are going smoothly. At times it seems easy to disclose to certain pleasant afriats personal feelings or opinions that should only be confided in our intimates. But positive afriats can and occasionally do turn on us very suddenly and become negative afriats. This can happen for a number of reasons. It happens when we find ourselves on different sides of an intra-afriational conflict, be it company politics or a personal conflict between co-afriats. It happens when the two afriats must rival for a better afriational position. It happens when two afriates fall in love with the same aspirat. It happens over borrowed money or possessions. It happens over falsehoods that one of the two afriats discovers and resents. It happens for a multitude of possible quarrels that human beings are capable of generating.

Disclosing confidentialities to afriats, even positive afriats, is risky for that reason. If the afriation becomes negative, the afriat we formerly treated as a friend may see little reason to feel responsible for safeguarding the confidentiality. Indeed, some aggravated afriats may seek revenge by disclosing secrets that may harm our status within the afriation or within our personal lives. I suspect that many of the scandalous "leaks" that surface in large corporations, government agencies, and other high-profile afriations are the result of someone mistaking a positive afriat for an intimate friend.

Remember, the litmus test for distinguishing between a positive afriat and a friend is the old question, "If the afriation were to disappear, would this person and I still seek each other's company to share common interests, activities, or affections?" If the answer is "I don't know," "probably not," or "maybe," consider said person a positive afriat. It's fine to be fond of positive afriats, but we should avoid divulging confidentialities to them. Afriations don't provide stable relationships. A positive afriat can quite quickly and unexpectedly become a negative afriat. Don't give them any ammunition.

Remember, an afriat is a person with whom we are forced to interact by an organization, institution, or a situation. A common afriational situation most of us occasionally face is the afriat who is a close friend, spouse, or "significant other" of a friend. Although there are times when we perceive these people as neutral or negative afriats, more often than not they tend to be positive afriats. Because they are friends or spouses of our friends, it's easy to think of these afriats as "friends" also and to entrust them with confidentialities that should be saved for our intimates.

This is dangerous. If our friend and his friend or spouse or "significant other" have a bitter falling out, which happens about half the time, our former positive afriat can and often does swiftly turn negative. Then we have an aggravated negative afriat knowing our potentially damaging confidentialities. Have you ever noticed how many witnesses in court cases are former positive afriats who were once friends of friends or spouses of friends of the defendant? They usually emerge as witnesses against people accused of such offenses as drug dealing, fraud, theft, or extortion. But law-abiding people can also suffer when their secrets "leak out" throughout the community. There are some things only our intimates, if anyone, should be told.

When trying to decide whether a spouse or a friend of a friend is also our friend or just our positive afriat, again we need to apply the old litmus test: "If our mutual friend should disappear, would this positive afriat and I still seek each other's company to share commonalities?" If the answer is anything but a confident "yes," then the person in question is not a friend but is a positive afriat. Love the afriat if you choose, but save your confidentialities for truly intimate friends.

Sometimes pidocas can create considerable discomfort in an afriation. That term, remember, is an acronym for a person in defiance of a categorical assignment. We encounter two types of pidocas in most large afriations of employment. We've already discussed one type, the afriats who mistake us for their enemies, who tend to be our aggravated negative afriats and our "bullies." I will have a little more to say about them in the next chapter.

The other type of pidocas we can always expect to encounter in a large afriation of employment are the afriats who continually endeavor to befriend us despite an obvious lack of common interests or activities. The more they pressure us, the stronger is the accompanying feeling of discomfort. Frequently, tactful but polite words to them don't serve much purpose, especially if they still bear their childhood conditioning that "we're all friends here." When this occurs, we are tempted to repel them with the behaviors of an aggravated negative afriat. Pidocas conditioned from youth to maintain a "friend or foe" mentality are then likely think of us as enemies and respond with an aggravated aggression of their own. Many of the affriational "bullies" I've observed are former pidocas seeking revenge against their former aspirats. I'll offer a little advice about how to repel persistent pidocas in the next chapter.

As I admitted earlier, the harms of afriations are hard to document. Some people have relatively few problems with their afriats, while others are continually miserable. I've conversed with many homeless people, and I've come to believe that many of them are in their existing state not because they are unwilling to work for a living, but because they psychologically cannot cope with being afriated.

But most of us exist somewhere in between the two extremes of being totally comfortable or absolutely miserable in our afriations. Based on my years of observation, the complaining that I constantly overhear, and surveys like the few I have cited, I'd say we're quite an afriat-troubled society. But this is something everyone needs to judge for him or herself. If you are content with your afriation, please feel fortunate. If you frequently feel troubled by your afriation, feel normal, and see if the next two chapters can help you entertain some ideas as to what you can do about it.

14

ADVICE FOR COPING WITH AFRIATS

This Chapter will be devoted to offering advice about afriats and afriations. If I am qualified to offer advice in this area, it is only because I am the first person to identify the concepts of afriation and because I've long observed people's behavior in reference to these concepts. I am not a professional counselor, doctor, behaviorist, or social scientist, and I admit to being afriationally opinionated.

Before offering any advice, it is important to acknowledge two things. First, not everybody in our society has afriats. The large majority of us certainly do, but there are people doing well living afriat-free. We'll discuss these people and our options for living without afriats in the next chapter.

Secondly, not everyone is overly dissatisfied with his or her present afriation. There are people, usually within smaller afriations, who find that all their afriats are positive. Such fortunate people may feel relatively comfortable in their afriations for years. The best advice I could offer them is the old adage, "If it's not broke, don't fix it. You must be doing something right." Perhaps these people are the ones who should be offering afriational advice.

In addition, there are people who seem resilient to negative afriats, people who can ignore gossip, irritation, and even harassment. They tend to be all business and try to stay out of other afriats' conflicts. They turn their cheeks to the afriation's bullies and try to concentrate on their tasks.

Another type of person who isn't bothered much by afriats reminds me of the lyrics to the song "Big John," popularized by Jimmy Dean in nineteen sixty-one:

"Every morning at the mine we'd see him arrive
He stood six foot six and weighed two forty-five

Kinda' broad at the shoulders and narrow at the hip
And every man knew you didn't give no lip
To Big John."

When I was a child, I always envied the Big Johns, the kids whose size and strength deterred all the schoolyard bullies. In large afriations of employment, you usually find a few Big Johns, men whose sheer size and strength is intimidating enough to make them immune to afriatioal bullying and even to passive aggressiveness. Occasionally, we also notice a few afriats who seem to carry themselves with a kind of dignity that commands respect. These folks are not only left unchallenged; they are often looked upon by their afriats as leaders.

But these few examples don't represent the majority of us who have afriats that we sometimes dread facing day after day. They certainly don't represent the large percentages of workers who cite "poor interpersonal relationships" as a major cause of their workplace stress. My advice is directed to the many people who are unhappy with their afriations.

There are people who are psychologically unequipped to tolerate being afriated at all. They include many of the recruits who are released from the military for being "unable to adjust" and many of the people who quit or who are fired from a series of jobs. They include many of the youths who drop out of school or are expelled, and they include many of the homeless who virtually drop out of society. It is my belief they include many of the people who commit suicide.

I don't know the reason why some people have more aversion to afriation than others. I don't know if anyone else can explain it. Most of us aren't troubled by it as severely as the examples I just mentioned, but our "normal" afriations do cause us noticeable and frequent stress. My advise to people who are troubled excessively by afriations is always, "Choose a life that doesn't require afriats. Take whatever risks and make whatever sacrifices are necessary to achieve that."

Some people consider that advice totally impractical. Others think of it as a long-term goal, but they believe that in the meantime, they need to continue being employed in their current afriations. Most of the advice I have to offer in this chapter is to people who would prefer to live with no afriats but who feel that for now afriation is a necessity.

This is the most important advice I can offer: *Don't allow your self-identity or sense of self-worth to come from an afriation.* Let them come from your interests, activities, and personal goals that are separate from your afriational responsibilities. Unfortunately, too many people don't have any personal goals or constructive off-duty activities. If that's the case with you, develop some interests and set some personal goals. Instead of telling yourself, "I'm a bartender," tell yourself, "I'm an oil painter who presently tends bar for a living." Instead of telling yourself, "I'm a store manager," tell yourself, "I'm a great family man, a jogger, and a photographer, and I also make my living managing a store." Instead of telling yourself, "I'm a machinist," tell yourself, "I'm a writer and a singer who currently makes a living operating machinery." This is the first step toward eliminating afriational frustration.

The second most important thing I can advise heavily afriated people is *find a healthy way to counter afriational stress*. Too often people resort to tobacco, alcohol, prescribed or illegal drugs, road rage, self or family abuse, network television, and other destructive practices to eliminate stress. If you are healthy, try something cardiovascular. Jogging after a stressful workday has always been my best weapon against stress. When I'm no longer physically able to run, I plan to learn some meditative practices that relieve stress. Working out on a heavy punching bag is one of the best stress eliminators I've experienced. Weight training, long-distance swimming, bike riding, and all known sports that stimulate the cardiovascular system are ideal practices. Some people find stress relief in playing musical instruments, painting, writing, dancing, acting, and other creative arts. Find what combats stress best for you and practice it after a stressful work shift.

The third most important thing I could advise someone is *be familiar with the nature of afriations*. When you first enter an afriation, remind yourself: "I have no friends here, yet and I have no enemies. We're all just afriats." Expect to encounter some positive afriats, some neutral afriats, and a few negative ones. Don't pressure any neutral afriats to accept you at first; remember, you must undergo the ritual of scrutiny that's characteristic of most afriations. Be a good listener, and always treat your afriats with courtesy, even those you perceive as negative.

Not everyone will agree with this, but I usually advise people to never take a position of co-management of an afriation. Afriational conflicts seem to inevitably arise from situations in which two or more people share the decision making and all the responsibilities. It's much better to be either the afriat who gives the orders or the afriat who follows the orders.

This is an important point, so allow me to reiterate it: *don't consider your negative afriats enemies*. Remember the litmus test: "If the afriation were to disappear, would this person still be trying to do me harm?" Normally, the answer is "no," illustrating that the person in question is a negative afriat. Avoid the temptation to hate the negative afriat. If you feel you need to hate something, hate your situation of being afriated and do something about it, as we'll discuss in the next chapter. It does no good to hate an aggravated afriat or to lower ourselves to his or her tactics of aggression.

There's an old proverb that declares, "It takes two to fight." I have never believed this proverb applies to incidents of bullying, but it makes sense in most other cases of afriational conflict. Simply refuse to go to war with an antagonistic negative afriat. Try to remain courteous, but speak to them only in the line of duty. When speaking to them is necessary, do it in a dutiful tone of voice and choose dutiful sounding words. Always stay out of disputes between other afriats, even if the dispute is about you.

In the event of a dispute with a negative afriat, don't insist on having the last word. Many quarrels between afriats would end quickly if one of the afriats would simply let the other have the last word. Too often neither is willing to drop the subject without having the last word. Let your afriat have the last word; it's not important.

If you make it clear to your negative afriat that you refuse to engage in a silly conflict, and if he or she persists with aggressive tactics, I'd say you're facing a case of bullying. Become well acquainted with the federal workplace harassment laws, because they prohibit bullying. However, it's important that you be able to document being bullied. Unfortunately, this may require the testimony of witnesses. You may find that many afriats are reluctant to volunteer as witnesses. I just advised you to stay out of conflicts between other afriats, and potential witnesses may be trying to follow that principle as well. If you can't positively document your allegations with witnesses, at least keep a written record of each account. Describe the incident thoroughly and record the time and date it occurred. That's a good enough start for some employers.

Once you are able to document a bullying incident, let the bullying afriat know that you can do so and that you intend to report the incident to the bully's administrators if it doesn't cease. If the administrators fail to act in your favor, or if the bully happens to be your supervising administrator, the harassment laws are written in your favor if you choose to initiate legal action. I've never been involved in such a lawsuit, but I understand there's good money these days in litigation, so you may gain financial rewards large enough to free you from the afriation.

As I suggested in the last chapter, confidentialities should only be divulged to our intimates. It's a bad practice to entrust intimate ideas or feelings to an afriat, even a very positive one. They are under no obligation to honor our confidence, and it's foolish to expect them to. Every time your secret is frequently repeated, it will begin with the words, "Don't tell anybody this, but...."

I'd further advise you not to allow any afriats to burden you with their confidentialities. If they are telling you their "secrets," they've likely told them to other afriats. Eventually the "secret" will fall upon the ears of some afriat who is not intended to hear it and the "betrayed" afriat may blame the nearest scapegoat who could well be you. Then you'll have an aggravated negative afriat who mistakes you for an enemy. I've seen that happen many times. When an afriat begins to relate personal "secrets," try to turn the conversation back to matters of the afriation. Speak in an official, business-like tone of voice.

In the interest of avoiding the creation of more aggravated negative afriats, I believe it's wise to never discuss one afriat with another. What you say about an afriat can quickly get around, and the contents can become quite twisted. If an afriat asks your opinion of another afriat, think of something nice to say and then quickly change the subject.

Unless the afriat is a very positive afriat and you feel you know him or her well enough to thoroughly trust, it's best to avoid lending afriats money or possessions. I learned this lesson as a very young soldier. The military's "Esprit de Corps" indoctrination about how the company is a "band of brothers" is a reissue of our primary school conditioning that "we're all friends here" and makes it easy to mistake military afriats for friends. I lost track of how many books, records, electric razors, and ten or twenty-dollar bills I was unable to recover from afriats I mistook for friends. I failed to apply the old litmus test: "If this army were to disappear, would these afriats and I seek each other's company to share mutual interests, activities, or affections?" In a few cases, the answer would have been "yes." They were not only the soldiers who were the easiest to collect debts from; they were the afriats who became my verified or intimate friends, the ones I am still in contact with today. But in general, it's best to avoid lending things to afriats.

I believe it's not advisable to accept favors from an afriat or to do anything that may lead the afriat to think you owe him or her a favor. The favor they demand in return is often reasonable, but sometimes they'll expect one that you feel a need to deny. Some afriats with a "friend or foe" mentality look upon this refusal as a betrayal and again you can quickly have an aggravated negative afriat who mistakes you for an enemy.

I've always advised afriated people to seek their friends and lovers outside of their afriations. However, I recognize that at times we all encounter an afriat who interests us enormously and who we feel compelled to know better. If you seek to befriend or date an afriat, it's best to let the progression be natural and gradual. This is especially true when considering romantic or sexual relationships. In life, when such a relationship goes sour, the normal thing to do is to stop seeing each other and to simply become each other's irrelevant. But if the involved parties are afriats, that choice is not an option. Hence you're stuck with another aggravated negative afriat and a tone of tense discomfort is added to the afriation.

Whatever you do, don't be anyone's pidoca. It's fine to approach an aspirat and acknowledge you have interests or activities in common that you'd like to share. If the aspirat declines your suggestion two or three times, it's best to seek friends or lovers elsewhere. Relentless pursuit of an aspirat can force him or her to adopt tactics intended to repel the pidoca. Modern afriations need less social tension, not more.

Of course, I've known people who've met their best friends or spouses through an afriation. On the other hand, I've known several women who dated afriats that they later decided to stop seeing. The pidocas persisted in their pursuits to the point of becoming stalkers, and required court-issued retraining orders to be kept at bay. One of these ladies urged me to add this to my list of suggestions: "Never take an afriat home or let one know where you live." I'll leave it to you readers to decide whether her advice sounds practical or overly harsh.

Fortunately, most pidocas don't require restraining orders. Some respond favorably to subtle hints. Others have to be addressed directly and told in so many words, "I'm absolutely not interested." When pidocas are so stubborn that direct words can't deter them, I have my own personal way to repel them. It may or may not work for you, but it has worked numerous times for me. Find out what religion, if any, the pidoca practices. Think of a religion that differs radically from the one the pidoca believes, tell your pidoca you do missionary work for that faith, and commence to try to convert him or her. That technique repels most stubborn pidocas, and it works just as well if not better on pidocas who are agnostics or atheists.

It's always been my belief that the phenomenon of afriation is unnatural to our species and should be considered one of mankind's major mistakes. The majority of modern Americans have simply come to take afriations for granted and to accept them as their fate. Yet there are people who do well without them. If afriations cause you more stressful discomfort than you are willing to accept, I'm sure you could find a way to live without them. The next chapter will focus entirely on the aspects of living without afriats.

15

LIVING WITHOUT AFRIATS

Those of us born during or shortly after World War Two were the last generation to grow up in a typical traditional mid-sized American town. In the mid-nineteen fifties, quaint little wooden or brick grocery stores were still located only two or three blocks apart in neighborhoods that were originally constructed for pedestrian traffic. The grocers and their families often lived in an apartment above or behind the store. Pedestrian-oriented, downtown business districts still included a multitude of small, family-owned businesses: tailor shops, barber shops, pet stores, "dime stores," department stores, drug stores, bars, small banks, quaint hotels, small office buildings housing a few lawyers, dentists, and insurance dealers, car dealerships, meat markets, produce markets, appliance stores, clothing stores, book stores, office supply stores, typewriter dealerships, furniture stores, small movie theaters, bicycle stores and toy stores, to mention only some.

Most of these businesses were still run by the people who owned them and required very few if any afriats. The only time we heard the word "manager" was in reference to the head coach of a baseball team. In the town where I grew up, most of the heavily afriated workers were employed by the smelter, the iron works, and the refinery. As it was in the early days of the industrial revolution, America's largest afriations were still the afriations of production, and World War II had thrown American production into high gear. My generation was the last to experience the American tradition of seeing product distribution in the hands of many small businesses.

Suddenly an economic shockwave hit every medium sized city in the U.S.A. By the mid-nineteen sixties, locally-owned, neighborhood groceries were almost extinct, and by the early seventies, the same fate was falling to most other small businesses. By the late nineteen seventies, most downtown business districts appeared "gutted out," and most of the surviving buildings housed pawn shops and thrift stores. By the mid eighties, huge office buildings owned by far away businesses towered where the smaller buildings had stood, and between these concrete and steel skyscrapers multi-storied parking garages were erected. It's astounding that a society can undergo such a drastic physical and social change in only three decades. It's also a classic example of how susceptible we are to our effectuals.

The economic shockwave that hit every "Hometown, U.S.A." in our land was, of course, the development of huge "chain store" oriented shopping centers. Small independent businesses, unable to compete with the prices of large-scale distribution, were quickly driven out of business, and formerly unafriated shopkeepers were forced to accept employment in large afriations. For the first time in the history of the Industrial Revolution, the distribution of products shifted from the hands of hundreds of local merchants to the hands of giant corporations with outlets housed in "malls." America's largest afriations are no longer her afriations of production, but are now her afriations of distribution.

In all of human history, the past five decades have represented the hardest times ever for a person to try to live without afriats. Even people who descend from generations of ranchers and farmers, unable to compete with large corporate food producers, have long been leaving their unafriated lives in the country to work in the afriations of the city. The large majority of Americans accept our afriated fates without question, feeling that the only way out is to work in one or more afriations for thirty or forty years until a monthly retirement check frees us from our afriations for the remainder of our short lives.

In a chapter dedicated to examining lives without afriats, a good place to begin is with the people I just mentioned, retirees. Afriations of employment are the most common of all afriations, of course, and unless a person is imprisoned, drafted, or young enough to be compelled to attend school, they are the only afriations that life's necessities compel people to accept. Pensioned retirees are perhaps the most obvious examples of people who no longer require the financial security of an afriation. A large percent of them have endured many years of difficult afriation, and they certainly merit their retirement. For most people, looking forward to a pensioned retirement is the strongest incentive to stay with an unfavorable afriation for many years. Other people decide that an unfavorable afriation is not an acceptable lifestyle and consider other alternatives, some of which we'll discuss shortly.

Like the independently wealthy, the retired are generally free to choose unafriated lives. I find it surprising how often the retired as well as the wealthy don't make that choice. The wealthy often prefer to become people's effectuals. As was the case in ancient times, modern effectuals still require afriats to carry out their practices. Retired people often join fraternal lodges, accept steady volunteer work, take post-retirement jobs, or make other choices that leave them reafriated. I believe such choices are often the result of a lifetime of afriational conditioning that makes some people unable to conceive of a life without afriats.

At the opposite end of the social-economic spectrum are people who have no afriats because they are willing to pay the price of being homeless. Of course, this is not true of all homeless people, but I've talked to many who prefer having no afriats and no home to having a home at the expense of having afriats. Most of the homeless people I've talked to know of places to eat free on a semi-regular basis and have found places, indoors or outdoors, to sleep. For this reason, they are not overly concerned about earning a paycheck. But what little money they do require has become harder to come by. Thirty years ago, many homeless people weren't doing bad just collecting empty aluminum cans and selling then to recycling centers, but soon they began to complain about too much competition from amateurs. The profession of "spare changing" people isn't as good as it used to be due to stricter solicitation laws, a population that carries credit cards more often than small currency, and a public that has grown weary of the homeless. Standing near the left turn lane of a busy intersection with a "Homeless Vet" sign has become the current prevailing occupation of many of our homeless irrelevants. At the time of this writing, I am not informed as to how lucrative this trade may be. Most intersection panhandlers are reluctant to tell irrelevants how much they "earn."

But I suspect that most of you readers are not wealthy, retired, or willing to live on the streets. Our question is this: In a time of massive, widespread afriation, what other options are available to working people who strongly desire a life without afriats?

The first step is to prepare ourselves mentally. We must accept the reality that initially, at least, we will most likely have to take some chances and make some sacrifices. Freedom from afriats may come at the price of financial security. For a while, we may have to sacrifice a higher income or even a regular paycheck. Financial plans for retirement and insurance for things like health care will become our own responsibilities. Failure or a series of failures may precede any financial success we may accomplish. We may be required to struggle against bleak odds. But we must believe in ourselves and expect to eventually succeed if we remain determined and persistent.

Unless you possess ample financial savings, simplify your life style to eliminate all nonessential expenditures. Don't become the super consumer that the modern media constantly urges you to be. Learn to distinguish between your wants and your needs, and keep your needs basic. Be satisfied with acquiring used necessities from yard sales or thrift stores, including clothing and utensils. Don't drive to places that are close enough to walk or bicycle to. Learn to live without using credit. Try to avoid all debt, a factor that forces many people to accept an afriated fate. Decide that the only money you will allow yourself to borrow is for a home or a business loan, and only when absolutely necessary. As I mentioned, an afriat-free existence may require considerable sacrifice.

When I talk to people who are determined to make their living in an unafriated way, I advise them to undertake what I refer to as the *double endeavor*. This involves our *primary endeavor* and our *secondary endeavors*. Our *primary endeavor* is our main goal. It is a long-term career we plan to pursue that will hopefully enable us to support our life's needs without afriats. It may be a practice that we can't begin for some time because it requires considerable training. It may require a college education or it may involve a period of individual study or practice. Whatever your choice is for a primary endeavor, most likely it will take planning, preparation, and development before it begins to support you financially. On the other hand, our *secondary endeavors* are the afriat-free activities intended to support us in the meantime.

Secondary endeavors are usually short-term, low paying, low prestige, unskilled tasks. It helps to reassure yourself that "somebody has to do it," and "at least I'm working without afriats." Many branches of the State Employment Office maintain a weekly list of people who want to be called for "spot jobs." Veterans normally have first preference, and people with "reliable transportation" are often most in demand. "Spot jobs" are typically one or two-day assignments that may or may not require you to work with others, but such limited exposure to these "temporary work colleagues" assures us they won't become afriats.

If our public employment offices could send us out on spot jobs frequently enough to enable us to support ourselves, these chores might be the only secondary endeavors we'd need as we prepared ourselves for our primary endeavor. In my experience, however, we can't rely entirely on public spot jobs for our minimal earnings. There may be periods of time when calls for workers are frequent, but there are often "dry periods" when very little temporary work is available. An unafriated temporary job seeker must supplement his or her employment agency's services by seeking short term, temporary jobs on his or her own. I will suggest some ideas shortly.

In addition to State Employment Agencies, privately owned labor agencies still exist. Three or four decades ago, these privately owned "temporary labor" agencies were a good option for people seeking to live without afriats. Their practice was to frequently call workers at home and offer them short-term job assignments. During periods of economic prosperity, one of these temporary agencies was often the only secondary endeavor a person might need. Today this is no longer the case.

In recent decades, two drastic changes have occurred in the nature of temporary work agencies. Almost half of them are now primarily interested in placing applicants in long-term afriations and do very little if anything about filling demands for short-term assignments. Most temporary work agencies that still accommodate short-term assignments no longer call workers by telephone. They now require their workers to come into a waiting room at four or five o'clock in the morning to sign up for a chance at a few hours work. The workers are required to wait there several hours until clients call for "temps." On some days, a given "temp" may be sent to a worksite by eight o'clock. On other days, he might sit in the waiting room until early afternoon when the dispatcher advises him to go away and return the next day. This existence doesn't seem to bother many of the homeless "temps" who have no better place to be at four o'clock in the morning than in a waiting room, but it's a waste of time for an ambitious person wishing to work on his or her primary endeavor. Such job agencies themselves tend to afriate their frequenters to the dispatcher and to other "temps" in the waiting room. Except for periods when you are desperate, it's best to avoid them.

Today it's much better for a person seeking short-term, unafriated work to develop a clientele of his or her own. Make an assessment of what skilled or unskilled services you have to offer, list them on a business card, and distribute them to any individuals or companies you suspect might some day be your clients. These activities can include anything from raking leaves and washing windows to typing and editing business reports. They can include anything from painting walls to making clothing alterations. Most communities now have small weekly publications that specialize in listing items for sale and services for hire. It's reasonably inexpensive to keep an ad for your services in these ad publications. Of course, many people nowadays find it to their advantage to advertise their services on an Internet web site.

If you are strong and in good health and appreciate a physical workout, go to all your local moving, transfer, and storage companies and ask to be placed on the "lumper list." "Lumper" is the trade name for a "temp" who is regularly or occasionally called in to help load or unload the huge trailers of "semi" trucks. It usually pays well for temporary work, and although your "co-workers" may become your occasionals, they won't be in your presence enough to become your afriats.

If you have a bachelor's degree from an accredited college or university, you can likely work as a substitute teacher for your secondary endeavor. If you want to remain free of afriats, don't accept any long-term teaching assignments. True, short-term substitute teachers can expect to have some stressful experiences, but at the end of a stressful workday, they can feel grateful that the most troublesome of the youths are not their afriats. Hence, they never need to take their stress home with them.

You can probably think of as many odd-job services as I can: trimming trees, clipping hedges, mowing lawns, moving households, painting, washing or changing windows, cleaning rain gutters and chimneys, changing motor oil, irrigating, digging gardens, delivering newspapers, hauling away trash, running errands and even walking people's dogs. If you have more sophisticated skills, use them whenever possible: teaching music lessons, tuning pianos, tuning bicycles or engines, trimming poodles, writing reports, tailoring fabrics, designing graphics, teaching karate, and repairing small appliances are several examples.

Remember, the low-paid, unskilled tasks that I've mentioned are presented as possible *secondary endeavors.* Their intent is to provide a little income while you learn to market your primary endeavor. Some people, however, choose primary endeavors that are not financially promising. Their goal may be to become as proficient as possible at one or more art forms, hoping their artistic passions will some day earn them a livelihood.

In 1926, the great western artist Charles M. Russell wrote, "Any man that can make a living doing what he likes is lucky, and I'm that. Any time I cash in now, I win." I cannot think of anyone I would consider more fortunate than the man or woman who makes a living marketing his or her own creations. If you have talents as a visual or performing artist, learn all you can about the possibility of marketing your creations.

Historically, the life of the artist has usually been a hard row to hoe. For generations, artists of all categories have been advised, "Don't give up your day job." Since the term "day job" suggests an afriation, let's rephrase that advice as, "Don't be too quick to abandon your secondary endeavor." Indeed, I've known many talented oil painters, musicians, writers, actors, and photographers who've worked at unskilled odd jobs all their lives because they never "made it" financially with their art. But they seldom harbor regrets. Most of them believe that people's lives are made rich by their creativities, not by their salaries. Most likely they couldn't have produced their best artwork if they'd lived under the stresses and pressures of a modern afriation.

I know very little about the current market for visual art. I've known a few painters who have made a living with their talent, but I've known a lot more who could never abandoned their secondary endeavors. The most financially successful painter I've met claims he earns between seventy and two hundred thousand dollars a year selling his work to museums and wealthy clients. He's told me that only about two percent of all visual artists succeed in "making it," and most of the others need to maintain their secondary endeavors for life.

I do know by experience that the marketing outlook for writers has been quite bleak these past four decades. Publishing companies have merged into huge conglomerates that are seldom willing to risk publishing a book by an "unknown author." People made famous by a notorious scandal are paid multimillion-dollar advances to sit down with a ghostwriter for a few hours and "write a book," while very good writers with important messages remain unpublished.

In the mid eighties, I thoroughly investigated the prospect of self-publication. It normally involved the author paying between eight and fourteen thousand dollars for a cellar full of books. Distribution was the writer's responsibility, and it was his biggest problem. Smaller, local bookstores blamed their reluctance to stock self-published books on their lack of space, and large chain bookstores claimed it was against company policy to display any books printed by a "vanity press." Frustrated by the lack of publishing opportunities, I stopped writing full-length books for twenty-one years.

I'm many years out of touch with household technology, but some other writers have informed me that today there are publishers who sell books on line and print them "on demand" as people chance upon them and order them via the internet. The writer doesn't have to ante up thousands of dollars in advance, and his cellar is free from boxes of books. I intend to try this style of marketing. If you are reading this book, you'll know this practice is working, at least for this writer. It sounds like a worthwhile experiment for the multitude of writers who have been denied publication opportunities.

In recent decades, the outlook has been just as bleak for professional musicians. A few decades ago, live music was still prevalent in theaters, restaurants, supper clubs, nightclubs, dance halls, grange halls, roadhouses, honkytonks, bars and dives throughout American. A few changes in technology later we find live music almost extinct. Recording opportunities have long been almost unobtainable for most good musicians and singers. The few performers chosen for the industry's cast of "stars" have long required strong financial backing, and in these days of silly music videos, they require movie star looks.

A few decades ago, self-producing a recording was an expensive proposition for most musicians. An investment of several thousand dollars resulted in a garage full of records that most record store managers would say they were not allowed to stock. Now recent developments in technology have made it possible for musicians to self-produce high fidelity recordings at low cost. I'm not familiar with the businesses personally, but I know musicians who talk of an on-line system of selling recordings that must be similar to the on-line marketing writers now use to sell books. New options appear to be emerging for people who deserve to record but who've been denied the opportunity.

Hopefully this might loosen some of the control that the large recording syndicates have long held over the industry.

Of course, a tiny fraction of a percent of artists, actors, performers, and writers strike it rich. Most of us don't. We've chosen a life of sacrifice. The daily stresses and distractions of an intense afriation would inhibit our creativities, so we must safeguard those secondary endeavors that support our artistic habits. The rewards we gain from our primary endeavors may not be ones we can put in the bank, but our lives will be richer because of them.

As we have discussed earlier, American corporations have been moving their afriations of production overseas and constructing huge afriations of distribution at home. Unable to compete, the majority of our small businesses have perished. Certainly we still see some small businesses operating— admirably, I'd say, considering the three to one odds against them. Lately, almost three quarters of new small businesses fold within five years. The competition of the large outlets intimidates a lot of us from even attempting to start our own business. Yes, it requires much courage to implement a business.

But a person dedicated to an unafriated life may want more from life than a string of menial odd jobs. I have the utmost respect for the adventurers who start their own businesses. I have no expertise—indeed, no experience—in the field of owning or operating a business. I can only present this outlook from my perspective as an interested social observer.

Basically, there are three types of small businesses. There are those that sell products, those that produce products, and those that sell services. In my general observation, the small businesses most likely to remain in operation for more than five years are those that provide services. Perhaps that's because the giant business conglomerates still haven't quite cornered the services market to the extent that they have cornered the products market. But corporate competition in the service industries is becoming increasingly fiercer, and I believe only the most competent of small businesses will survive.

A good example of that theory is seen in the auto repair business. A few decades ago, my hometown, like most medium-sized American cities, had a large number of small auto repair shops, mostly owned and operated by one individual with one or two hired mechanics. Soon their effectuals began to install more and more computerized technology into new cars. Manufacturers insisted that the cars should be serviced only in the large shops owned by the car dealerships. Some of the small shops survived by specializing in the repair of older models. Some were eventually able to meet the cost of the newly required technology and survived. The majority of them folded and many of the small shop mechanics had to accept employment in large automotive afriations. I've noticed that the small auto shops that have survived have abnormally good mechanics. A few I know locally are so good they can determine what's wrong with an engine's performance by just listening to it. They do great work and complete it in good time. Their services aren't cheap, but they're extremely efficient. These men are a vanishing breed.

I've noticed the same can be said about most of today's other small businesses that are involved in building, installing, or repairing things, including electronic technicians, plumbers, furnace and air conditioning specialists, fencers, driveway and garage contractors, and house remodelers, to name just a few. Those businesses that survive more than five years in this global economy have had to become very professionally competent. Become very good at your trade if you intend to start a small business.

Of the three types of small businesses, I've noticed that those that sell products instead of services have the least chance of lasting five years. The reason, of course, is that small business simply can't produce or market products as cheaply as the large conglomerates. We would be foolish to try to open a store that sold the exact same items as the ones for sale in every shopping center and mall. If a person wants to live unafriated by starting a business that produces or sells something, he needs to produce and/or sell items that are more unique or are of better quality than the mass-manufactured products of American-owned afriations overseas.

I've known people who handcraft much finer stringed musical instruments than factories can manufacture, including violins, mandolins, harps, and acoustic guitars. Their instruments cost considerably more than factory-made brands, but somewhere in the global economy buyers are likely to be found for them, often on line. I've met other people who hand make fine furniture, high quality archery bows and arrows, shaps and saddles, personally fitted boots, rifles, belts, curtains, animal skin rugs, and many other items that are of considerably higher quality than that of their factory-produced counterparts. They sell their products to connoisseurs, and although they don't do a large volume of business, they tend to stay in business longer than small businesses selling conventional, factory-made products.

Some people have found a market producing and/or vending items of average quality that are desired because they are unique. I once met an oil painter of below-average talents who couldn't sell a painting to his parents. Soon he had more orders than he could fill when he began to paint western scenery on old round saw blades. I knew a photographer of less than average talents who found he could make a good living indeed selling tourists photos of themselves wearing late nineteenth century western apparel. I know a woman who makes and sells quilts with embroideries of her clients' pets on the fabrics. I know a fellow who makes and sells knives with hand-engraved buffalo and Indians on the bone handles. These are just a few examples of unique items to sell that aren't "made in Korea."

The old business adage "find a need and fill it" still pertains. If you're determined to work for yourself without afriats, examine your community and see what needs exist that you can fill. Remember, we live in an incredibly fast changing society. The people who gain the most are likely to be the people who aptly foresee the needs of the near future.

Finally, a person interested in an unafriated career might consider an independent practice in one of the "highly paid" professions. I've never held a college degree higher than a B.A. and I've known relatively few dentists, doctors, attorneys, therapists, or councelors. That doesn't qualify me to write much on the subject. Anyone interested in learning a modern profession would be wise to discuss the feasibility of practicing that profession independently with someone already attempting it. I realize that some of these self-employed professionals may need to hire a small number of assistants such as secretaries, paramedics, or receptionists, but chances are the professional would have the option of filling these positions with known friends rather than afriats. Even when some of the staff members are afriats, the afriation is small and most likely positive, and it is always under the control of the hiring professional.

As with craftsmen in the skilled trades, a self-employed professional may never achieve the higher pay scale of his afriated counterparts. We live in such a litigation-oriented society that some of the doctors I've talked to expressed that malpractice suits against physicians have driven up the cost of their insurance to the extent that doctors are leaving their small practices for the security of large clinical afriations. I've been told that these and other costs involved in operating a private practice make it hard for a self-employed practitioner to earn what he or she might earn being employed by a hospital, clinic, or HMO. However, this is not always the case. Two doctors have told me that they realized more earnings after leaving a large medical afriation to start their own practice. One of them felt that stress was more prevalent in a private practice due to the pressures involved in administering a business.

In recent decades, of course, the medical profession has become quite specialized. More than one doctor has told me that a physician's income may depend more on his or her specialty than on the factor of self employment vs. afriational employment. For example, a neurosurgeon is among the highest paid of medical doctors and a pediatrician is among the lowest paid. A person who desires to practice medicine independently without sacrificing large earnings would need to learn which high paying specialties can best be practiced privately.

People following the medical profession have also told me that the type of insurance their patients carry can be a larger factor in determining a doctor's income than the factor of self employment vs. hospital or clinical employment. Of course, some insurance plans pay more than others for the same kind of treatment, and in general, private insurance pays more than Medicare. A person wanting to practice medicine independently without sacrificing income potential might be advised to look for a specialty which caters to a clientele of privately insured occasionals.

Although there are many factors that determine a doctor's income, more physicians than not that I've questioned have indicated that a doctor would normally expect to earn less in a private practice. Like the small businessman, the artist, the craftsman, and the laborer, most self-employed physicians might need to accept lower earnings as a condition for less afriation. It's a matter of what the individual professional values more.

I know several attorneys who have been both self-employed and employed by large law firms, and they all believe that most attorneys can earn considerably more income these days working for the large law afriations, especially attorneys newly out of law school. Once an attorney has acquired experience, a reputation, and a clientele, of course, his or her potential for earnings in a private practice may become as great as or greater than that of his or her counterparts employed by a law firm. One or two lawyers I've questioned indicated that their earnings increased when they left a law firm to establish a private practice. But in general, I'm told, the F. Lee Baileys and the Johnny Cochrans are the exceptions. "Most private-practice attorneys don't earn nearly as much as the public wants to believe," a retired attorney told me. "There's a lot more competition in the legal business now than there was when I started." Most of the lawyers I questioned expressed that the highly afriated attorneys can normally expect higher earnings.

A former highly afriated attorney who now makes an unafriated living trimming trees told me, "If you work for a big law firm, they own your life, especially if you're new to the firm. That's when they expect you to be their research puppy. They think nothing of demanding that you work twelve to sixteen hours a day, sometimes six or seven days a week, for those fat salaries." I don't know enough about the legal profession to know if that's the exception or the norm. A student interested in practicing law needs to ask questions of some successful practitioners. But as with most other walks of life, loss of some income and security may be the price an attorney often pays to be relatively unafriated. It takes fortitude, sacrifice, and determination to exist without afriats, but some people's constitutions require that they try.

Earlier I advised, "Avoid all debt." One of the few exceptions to that rule is a business loan. It's justified if it enables us to start a career that frees us of afriations. My advice to artists was, "Don't be too quick to abandon your secondary endeavors," but to a self-employed small businessman I'd say, "Cut yourself loose from your secondary endeavors as soon as possible and put all your time and energy into the new business."

I am thirty years out of touch with household technology, but I am aware that more and more people are making a living by conducting business transactions and investments via the computer. I'm told this will be the norm in the near future, and I suppose it will be. I'm not entirely comfortable with the concept, but one obviously favorable result is it should eliminate afriats for a lot of people. People who don't adapt well to afriations should be and probably are exploring their on-line possibilities.

But even if most buying and selling become conducted via the Internet, this is still the bottom line: the products bought and sold must first be produced and distributed. We've seen our nation physically and socially transformed to accommodate mass production, and now it's being transformed again to accommodate mass distribution. Mass afriation is the inevitable by-product, always necessary to an industrialized or technological society. Most people who live relatively unafriated lives do so, to varying degrees, at the expense of our afriated humanity. There is room for only a limited number of unafriated workers in a modern society, so expect stiff competition, and become highly competent at what you choose.

Thank you for reading this dissertation. Many people who read its contents raise the same questions and objections. In anticipation of some specific questions, I have included a last chapter of "commonly asked questions and answers." If Chapter Sixteen still leaves you with unanswered questions or objections, feel free to address them Email to richardbakerbird@yahoo.com.

16

COMMONLY ASKED QUESTIONS

QUESTION: Can a person belong to more than one of the seven interactional categories simultaneously?

ANSWER: Only very rarely. Normally, if we reclassify someone, we should think of him or her as a member of the new category only. For example, if an irrelevant, occasional, or afriat becomes our friend, we should think of him or her as a friend and no longer a member of the previous category. The same holds true for an irrelevant, an occasional, or an afriat whom we reclassify as an enemy.

The very few exceptions to this principle that I can think of all involve the category enemies. An effectual who would maliciously and intentionally harm us would also be our enemy. A prime example of an *effectual enemy* would be Osama Bin Laden. The attacks he organized against the United States on September 11, 2001, have greatly affected the lives of all Americans ever since. Of course, he would intentionally do us harm at any opportunity simply because we are Americans. He is both an enemy and an effectual. Adolph Hitler was another classic example of an *effectual enemy*. Fortunately, these individuals are so rare that they don't merit being considered a major interactional category.

As I mentioned previously, an antagonistic afriat should be reclassified as an enemy if the answer is "yes" to the litmus test question, "If the afriation were to disappear, would this afriat still be trying to do me harm?" More often the answer is "no," meaning the aggravated person is a negative afriat. But suppose a person who has previously been our enemy becomes a member of an afriation to which we belong, such as an afriation of employment? In this case, I'd tend to think of this new afriat as an *afriat enemy*. These individuals are also far too rare to merit being considered an interactional category.

Someone whom we meet only once who intentionally does us long-term harm might be thought of as both an enemy and a single-contact influential. With the exception of these three rare examples, we should assign most individuals to one interactional category at a time.

QUESTION: How would you classify family members and other relatives?

ANSWER: The classification of family members can be a sensitive topic, and it's one I'd prefer to avoid. However, this question is asked of me so frequently that I've had to give it considerable thought.

Ideally, a family should be and often is a sacred institution of close-knit, verified friends and loving intimates. Unfortunately, this is not always the case. Two siblings who constantly quarrel and who wouldn't associate with each other much if they didn't share the same parents could be thought of as afriats. A husband and wife who no longer love each other but who stay married for the sake of their children might also be considered afriats. A married couple undergoing a bitter divorce, especially if it's accompanied by a custody lawsuit, can be thought of as enemies. Two siblings who oppose each other in a lawsuit over an inheritance can also become quite bitter enemies.

Cousins that we never see and wouldn't recognize in an encounter might as well be thought of as irrelevants. If we see them occasionally and acknowledge them at family reunions or in public places, they would be occasionals. Close siblings, cousins, aunts, uncles and grandparents that we've always loved but seldom see anymore because of distance should be thought of as old friends. Normally, our aging parents or our grown sons and daughters that we don't see very often because of distance remain our verified friends, and perhaps our intimates. Parents and offspring have been known to have a falling out and "disown" each other. In such cases, they may become irrelevants or even enemies.

In short, assigning relatives to an interactional category is really no different from making these assignments to people who aren't relatives. The same litmus test applies: "If it weren't for the institution of our family, would we still seek each other's company to share common interests, activities, or affections?" Or perhaps this question would sometimes better apply: "If it weren't for the family, would we still be quarrelling?"

But I prefer to not classify relatives as anything but parents, sons, daughters, brothers, sisters, cousins, uncles, aunts, nieces, nephews, grandparents, etc. Many of us tend to think of the family as a sacred institution and the classifying of family members can be an overly touchy subject.

QUESTION: Do most people agree with or disagree with your classifications, categories, and philosophies?

ANSWER: Most people seem to agree with most of my classifications and principles. Some people don't agree that being afriated to a number of people is a major problem. That's because afriations vary largely and the effect of an afriation varies from person to person. Some people feel relatively comfortable among their afriats. Other people find their contacts very stressful.

QUESTION: Isn't your analysis of the social order a little cold, unfriendly, and anti-social?

ANSWER: I believe such a perception is in the eye of the beholder. I always feel sad to hear that question, for nothing I have written is intended to be cold, unfriendly, or antisocial. I have advised everyone to always treat occasionals and afriats with respect and courtesy, even negative afriats. I encourage people to value friends, especially verified friends and intimates. I urge people not to mistake negative afriats for enemies, but to try to understand them. I encourage people to be helpful to irrelevants in trouble. No, I don't think I'm advocating an unfriendly or antisocial philosophy.

Perhaps it is my advice "don't mistake afriats for friends" that objectors find cold or antisocial, especially people who have the good fortune of having pleasant, positive afriats. Don't misconstrue my advice. Certainly be "friendly" and pleasant to your positive afriats and like them as much as they like you. Perhaps your mutual affections will become strong enough to establish a friendship. Perhaps common interests and activities will soon foster a friendship. When in doubt, follow the litmus test. Ask yourself, "If it weren't for this afriation, would this pleasant positive afriat and I still voluntarily get together to share commonalities?" If the answer is "not yet," continue to like the afriat, of course, but follow the precautions I have outlined. Don't confide in him or her, avoiding lending him or her things, don't ask the afriat for favors, and realize that any afriated relationship can prove very unstable.

QUESTION: Could it be that this whole ideology is simply a mental defense mechanism?

ANSWER: It certainly is in part. Of course, we can't blame a person for wanting to defend him or herself against afriats, effectuals, enemies, or pidocas. But it's much more than just a defense mechanism. It's a convenient tool for analyzing our social order and everyone's interactional role toward us. It's a handy code in deciding how to react to the behavior of individuals from the various categories.

QUESTION: With such an overly cautious approach toward afriats, how do you ever expect friendships to develop?

ANSWER: No matter how cautious or reckless you may be toward new afriats, no real friendship is ever going to develop without common interests, activities, or affections. Remember, an afriation in itself can't cause friendships. It can only expose us to potential friends. If the commonalities exist, often a friendship will naturally develop. Approach your aspirat tactfully and unthreateningly, acknowledge your common interests, and hope that initiates a friendship. If the aspirat is reluctant to befriend you, don't become his or her pidoca.

QUESTION: Could civilization exist without afriations?

ANSWER: Possibly. Throughout most of civilization's brief history, most people lived with no afriats. Originally, afriations were a phenomenon of the ruling class, and were limited to people who were slaves, servants, prisoners, or soldiers.

A civilization entirely void of afriations would require two conditions: first, a simple social-economic system like those of preindustrialism, and second, an absence of rulers wanting to afriate people into armies and prisons. I know some very aware people who believe that the first of these two conditions will inevitably happen, but I don't know anyone who believes the second is likely to happen.

If somehow these two conditions were to come about, our next question would logically be, "Would a civilized society always need jails to detain and punish its social offenders?"

Native American societies didn't have jails. If a brave committed an offense against the tribe, he would be given the opportunity to plead his case before the tribal elders judging him. Then he would be instructed to wait in solitude away from the tribe while his elders decided on his appropriate punishment. Native Americans have told me that the accused would never flee, and that he would accept his torment "without a whimper."

I don't know to what extent that belief is historically accurate. The most plausible reason why aboriginal Americans had no prisons was their nomadic, migratory existence. They relied on banishment, corporal punishment, and in severe cases, capital punishment to enforce their social mores. It seems a civilization with a simple social-economic system could exist without jails only if it relied heavily on corporal and capital punishment to preserve law and order.

QUESTION: Could an industrial, technological society exist without afriations?

ANSWER: Of course not, especially a consumer-oriented society such as ours. Modern economies rely on standardized mass production. Although American corporations have been steadily transplanting their afriations of production to formerly unindustrialized countries, large, standardized afriations of distribution keep springing up everywhere, providing afriated employment to many of the afriats displaced by factory closures.

The more "high tech" a product is, the more it requires being mass-produced in large afriations. The American public is having an enormous and incredible romance with electronics. Any new contrivance our effectuals throw our way is bound to be purchased by millions of overly faithful consumers who hardly know their wants from their needs. Our large afriations of distribution certainly mirror modern society's values.

QUESTION: Why do you feel that most people who live largely unafriated lives do so to a large extent at the expense of afriated people?

ANSWER: Because they most often require tools, parts, or other goods produced by afriations. For an example, suppose a person owns a small bicycle repair business and works alone without afriats. He relies on afriations of production to manufacture tools and parts, to say nothing of the bikes themselves. The same could be said about most anyone who makes a living repairing, installing, or building things or providing any other service that relies on factory produced items. A person who makes an unafriated living marketing things on the internet relies on afriations to produce what he sells, to say nothing of producing the computer components he uses.

I've known a few unafriated people who make a good living giving motivational lectures or professional development speeches to employees of businesses, government agencies, and school systems. Of course, they rely on having bodies of afriated people to attend the lecture. Similarly, a licensed teacher who chooses to work as a substitute to avoid having afriats relies on the afriated teachers who periodically need filling in for, to say nothing of afriated children and administrators. Self-employed, unafriated tradesmen, craftsmen, professionals, and even visual and performing artists most always rely on supplies produced by large afriations. Only a person who produces and sells services or products without the use of materials or tools created in afriations could boast of *not* being unafriated at afriated people's expense. And even these very autonomous people would likely depend on afriated people to purchase their products or services.

QUESTION: Why do you believe there is room for only a limited number of unafriated workers is a modern, technological society?

ANSWER: This is true for three reasons. First, as I just discussed, unafriated people in a modern society almost always require supplies produced by afriations. If everyone lived unafriated lives, who would produce the supplies? Second, the demand for any given product or service has its limits. For example, there is a demand for only a small number of unafriated bike repairmen in a society attached to motor vehicles. There is a demand for only a limited number of self-employed auto mechanics in a system where automotive repairs increasingly need to be done in the dealerships' shops. There is a demand for relatively few independent garment makers when most people buy mass-manufactured clothes in shopping malls. Third, competition is fierce for people wanting to run a small, unafriated business. Only people who are the most determined and become the most competent are likely to succeed.

QUESTION: Do you think mankind as a whole will ever return to a largely unafriated existence?

ANSWER: I believe this will eventually prove inevitable. I am certainly no authority on our planet's ecology, but it's common knowledge that the western world's industrial and automotive economies have put stresses on our Earth that by now may be irreparable. This effect is about to multiply as the world's most populated countries including China and India continue to modernize and industrialize. I fear that mankind must voluntarily return to simpler social-economic systems of limited production and consumption, or nature will force such a return. Man-made or natural catastrophes might even force mankind to return to the nomadic tribal lives that humans lived throughout most of our history. Our Earth simply can't continue to support our present practice of unchecked production and consumption.

QUESTION: This is a unique and interesting way of looking at our social order, and perhaps there is some truth to it. But without sufficient studies to support your assertions, don't we have to question the validity of some of your premises?

ANSWER: Certainly. While writing this book, I often asked myself, "Do I really know what I'm talking about, or is this just the babbling of a sentimental, antisocial old fool?"

As I've admitted previously, these ideas are all based upon a few decades of personal observation and interpretation. No two people perceive anything quite the same, so I'd expect to find some people with an entirely different perception and interpretation of society's interpersonal interactions. Surprisingly, however, the large majority of people to whom I present these theories feel most of the principles are valid, based on their personal experiences with afriations.

If I expected to live considerably longer, I would begin to conduct some controlled research to verify my theories, but I am no longer young. Anyone else is certainly welcome to conduct any surveys that might prove or disprove my statements. But, of course, this is too much to expect of a person who is just mildly curious. I'd simply advise any curious party, "Observe for yourself." Take notice of your relationships with people and decide for yourself if the categories and principles I've presented apply to you. Maybe this is another book that "isn't for everybody." Many people, however, have told me they have found these concepts to be highly useful tools for mentally sorting out their relationships and for deciding how to interact with various members of the seven interactional categories.